YORK NOT

KV-446-183

York Notes Rapid Revision

Animal Farm

AQA GCSE English Literature

Written by Keith Brindle

Pears

YORK
PRESS

9030 00007 0090 1

YORK PRESS
322 Old Brompton Road, London SW5 9JH

PEARSON EDUCATION LIMITED
80 Strand, London, WC2R 0RL

© Librairie du Liban *Publishers* 2019

10 9 8 7 6 5 4 3 2 1

ISBN 978–1–2922–7098–2

Phototypeset by DTP Media
Printed in Slovakia

LONDON BOROUGH OF WANDSWORTH		
9030 00007 0090 1		
Askews & Holts	09-Jan-2020	
823.912	£3.99	
	WW19015055	

Text credits:
Animal Farm by George Orwell (copyright © George Orwell, 1945). Reproduced by permission of Bill Hamilton as the Literary Executor of the Estate of the late Sonia Brownell Orwell and Secker & Warburg Ltd.
Excerpts from ANIMAL FARM by George Orwell. Copyright 1946 by Sonia Brownell Orwell; copyright © renewed 1974 by Sonia Orwell. Reprinted by permission of Houghton Mifflin Harcourt Publishing Company. All rights reserved.
Excerpts from Animal Farm by George Orwell, reproduced by permission of the Estate of the late Sonia Brownell Orwell, 1987. Reproduced by permission of Penguin Books Ltd.

Photo credits:
GL Archive/Alamy for page 4 top / Elflaco1983/Shutterstock for page 6 top and 26 top / symbiot/ Shutterstock for page 8 middle / Unkas Photo/Shutterstock for page 10 top / PhotoSongserm/ Shutterstock for page 12 middle / mediaphotos/© iStock for page 14 bottom / dancingfishes/© iStock for page 16 middle and page 30 top / Akademie/Alamy for page 20 top / Granger Historical Picture Archive/Alamy for page 22 top / 2checkingout/Shutterstock for page 24 top / Alessandro Carnevale/Shutterstock for page 25 bottom / Anek Sakdee/© iStock for page 28 top / daseaford/ Shutterstock for page 32 top / Paul Maguire/Shutterstock for page 34 top / Olga_i/Shutterstock for page 36 top / Angyalosi Beata/Shutterstock for page 36 middle / Ariel Celeste Photography/ Shutterstock for page 38 middle / flashgun/Shutterstock for page 38 bottom / LENblR/© iStock for page 42 middle / Tana888/Shutterstock for page 44 bottom / Alexander Sviridov/Shutterstock for page 46 middle / Tithi Luadthong/Shutterstock for page 48 middle / nuwatphoto/Shutterstock for page 50 middle / Grigorita Ko/Shutterstock for page 52 bottom / Madlen/Shutterstock for page 56 bottom / Anze Mulec/Shutterstock for page 58 middle / Maya Kruchankova/Shutterstock for page 60 middle / gabriel12/Shutterstock for page 61 bottom

CONTENTS

INTRODUCTION Who was George Orwell?

Three key things about George Orwell

1. He was born in 1903 in **India** and went to **Eton**.
2. Despite his relatively **privileged upbringing**, he championed the poor and downtrodden.
3. His most famous books are **Animal Farm**, an allegory about Communism, and **Nineteen Eighty-Four**, his vision of a grim future world.

Why did Orwell write *Animal Farm*?

● He wrote *Animal Farm* in 1945 to reflect the events leading to the **Russian Revolution** and the Stalinist era which followed.
● He wanted to show how people's hopes for a better life were ruined by Stalin's **brutal dictatorship**.
● When the book was published, the UK was an ally of Stalin's Soviet Union, and Orwell wanted to show why this was wrong.

What points does Orwell make in the novel?

● He shows how Napoleon, who **represents Stalin**, gradually takes complete control of the farm, helped by Squealer's propaganda.
● Because the animals are so easily fooled, he generates sympathy for them. The reader feels especially for Boxer, a representative of the **working class**.
● By the end, we see that nothing is any better for the animals – if anything, life has been worse under Napoleon's rule. Everything returns to the way it was in the beginning.

How was the novel received?

● At first, Orwell had trouble getting it published.
● After it was published, international relations changed and there was a 'Cold War' with the Soviet Union. The novel then became a huge success.
● It was listed as 46th most popular novel in the BBC's 'Big Read' survey in 2003, and was on *Time* magazine's list of the 100 best modern English language novels.

Chapters 1 and 2

- Old Major holds a meeting to tell the animals about his dream of their lives free from slavery.
- He explains that mankind is the cause of all their problems. He sings the revolutionary song 'Beasts of England' to them.
- After Old Major's death, the pigs prepare and organise the other animals for the Rebellion.
- Jones is driven out, and the Seven Commandments are written on the barn.
- Snowball, Napoleon and Squealer become the leaders.

Chapters 3 and 4

- The harvest is gathered successfully.
- Snowball tries to educate the animals; Napoleon trains the puppies.
- Jones is beaten in the Battle of the Cowshed.
- Snowball and Boxer lead the animals to victory.

Chapters 5 and 6

- Napoleon drives Snowball from the farm and behaves like a tyrant.
- Sunday debates are abolished and the first commandment is broken.
- Napoleon, protected by his dogs, changes policy, including trading with other farms.
- Napoleon says Snowball's windmill will be built, but it falls down.

Chapters 9 and 10

- The pigs lead a life of luxury and become human in their vices.
- When Boxer can no longer work he is sold for meat, and we empathise with his plight.
- The commandments become 'All animals are equal but some animals are more equal than others'.
- Symbolically, Animal Farm reverts to the name Manor Farm.
- The action ends with the animals outside looking into the farmhouse as the pigs dine with the local human farmers.

Chapters 7 and 8

- The animals work harder than ever and face starvation.
- Napoleon executes his opponents; the animals are terrified and confused.
- The windmill is rebuilt but then destroyed by Frederick.
- Boxer and Napoleon drive out the humans at the Battle of the Windmill.

Five key things about Chapters 1 and 2

These chapters establish the **characters** and set out key **themes** in the novel.

1. Before he dies, **Old Major** tells the other animals about **his dream** of a better life: although the novel is about animals, it is an **allegory** that deals with what happened in the **Russian Revolution** and its **aftermath**.

2. The animals are introduced. **The pigs**, the cleverest, prepare for the **Rebellion**.

3. **Napoleon**, **Snowball** and **Squealer** become the **leaders**.

4. When **Jones**, a lazy drunk, is driven out, the pigs present the **Seven Commandments**, based on what Old Major said. They are the principles by which the animals will live.

5. Snowball is the **obvious leader** but Napoleon **behaves suspiciously**. The reader suspects all might not be perfect in the future: are the pigs corrupt too? Orwell **foreshadows** what is to come.

What happens in Chapter 1?

- Old Major presents his **philosophy** of life to a **meeting** of the animals. He attacks mankind for exploiting them.
- He explains his dream of a **better future** and teaches the animals the words to 'Beasts of England'.
- Mr Jones's violent nature is demonstrated when he **fires his gun** to silence the animals in their meeting: he **'let fly a charge of number 6 shot'**.

What happens in Chapter 2?

- The pigs develop Animalism: the horses, Boxer and Clover, are its most loyal followers.
- Mr Jones is driven out, and the Seven Commandments, setting out the basis of Animalism, are painted on the barn and **'could be read thirty yards away'**. The pigs have learned the human skills of reading and writing.
- Snowball enthusiastically calls the animals to work harder for a brighter future. Napoleon takes charge of the milk.

Five key quotations

1. The basis of Animalism: **'All animals are equal.'** (Chapter 2)

2. Snowball has an attractive personality: **'Snowball was a more vivacious pig than Napoleon, quicker in speech and more inventive'** (Chapter 2)

3. Napoleon is different: **'Napoleon was a large, rather fierce-looking Berkshire boar ... with a reputation for getting his own way.'** (Chapter 2)

4. The horses are devoted to the revolution: **'Their most faithful disciples were the two cart-horses, Boxer and Clover.'** (Chapter 2)

5. The Seven Commandments become absolute law: **'an unalterable law by which all the animals on Animal Farm must live for ever after'** (Chapter 2)

Note it!

Notice how the Seven Commandments are altered as the novel progresses, so that life on the farm reverts to the way it was when Jones was in charge.

Exam focus

How can I write about foreshadowing in these chapters? (AO1)

You can focus on the characters and the themes of freedom and equality.

> Because the novel begins with Old Major's dream, the reader realises his ideas will be central to what follows. The opening of the novel is generally positive, and when he says, 'All animals are equal' it seems that this philosophy of equality is what the animals will seek to follow – though when Napoleon appears to take charge of the milk, this foreshadows what happens later.

Topic sentence introduces point
Embeds appropriate quotation
Explains its importance
Develops the point further

Now you try!

Finish this paragraph about how the pigs take charge from the beginning. Use one or two of the quotations from the list.

After Old Major dies, Snowball seems set to become leader as he has the most appealing personality . . . .

My progress   Needs more work ☐   Getting there ☐   Sorted! ☐   7

PLOT AND STRUCTURE Chapters 3 and 4

Five key things about Chapters 3 and 4

In these chapters, **Animal Farm develops**. We see the differences between the animals, Snowball and Napoleon disagree in the debates, and the humans are defeated when they try to recapture the farm.

1. The animals are happy and work hard together to complete the **harvest**, though **the pigs** seem to have an **easier life** than the others.
2. We see the **importance of Boxer** to the farm's success.
3. The **differences** between the lead pigs are clearer: Snowball tries to **educate** all the animals; Napoleon says the young are **most important**.
4. The **humans** try to take back **control** of the farm but the animals **fight back**, and Snowball and Boxer lead them to victory.
5. **Boxer** becomes an even more **sympathetic** character because he is sorry for hurting the stable-lad.

What happens in Chapter 3?

- The first harvest is completed in record time: the animals work while the pigs **'directed and supervised the others'**.
- Snowball and Napoleon lead the Sunday debates but always disagree.
- Snowball sets up committees and tries to teach the animals to read and write.

- Napoleon takes the puppies away from their mothers to educate them himself.
- Squealer defends the pigs' actions when it is found they have taken the apples and milk. He says it is so that they can be healthy and run the farm better.

What happens in Chapter 4?

- The animals try to spread their revolutionary ideas across the countryside.
- Mr Jones, supported by men from Pinchfield and Foxwood farms, tries to retake the farm but ends up **'in ignominious retreat'**.
- Snowball, supported by Boxer, leads the animals to victory in the Battle of the Cowshed. They are both awarded a medal: **'Animal Hero, First Class'**.

Five key quotations

1. Boxer works hardest to get the harvest in: **'the entire work of the farm seemed to rest upon his mighty shoulders'** (Chapter 3)

2. Snowball and Napoleon almost always disagree: **'whatever suggestion either of them made, the other could be counted on to oppose it'** (Chapter 3)

3. Snowball makes the idea of Animalism easier for the less intelligent animals: **'Four legs good, two legs bad.'** (Chapter 3)

4. Boxer is upset when he thinks he has killed the stable-lad: **'I have no wish to take life, not even human life'** (Chapter 4)

5. Snowball is unsentimental: **'The only good human being is a dead one.'** (Chapter 4)

Note it!

Snowball and Napoleon are different in their tactics: notice how Snowball seems important to begin with, but as Napoleon takes control he changes how Snowball is viewed, even altering the animals' shared memories of what he achieved.

Exam focus

How can I write about the structure? AO2

You can show how the pigs gradually take more control.

As the story develops, we see how the pigs set up a kind of hierarchy. The other animals do the hard work while the pigs merely supervise and get more rewards, such as apples and milk. Snowball presents himself as leader by teaching the animals (for example, simplifying Animalism to 'Four legs good, two legs bad'), while Napoleon appears to work in the background, taking away the puppies from their mothers and supervising their education.

Topic sentence introduces the point	
Point is explained further	
Quotation effectively embedded	
Relevant detail added	

Now you try!

Finish this paragraph about how Boxer is presented sympathetically, in contrast to the pigs. Use one or two of the quotations from the list.

Boxer fights bravely in the Battle of the Cowshed, but does not want to harm anyone and is distraught because...

PLOT AND STRUCTURE Chapters 5 and 6

Five key things about Chapters 5 and 6

In Chapters 5 and 6, the mood darkens as Napoleon takes control and the aims of the revolution begin to fail.

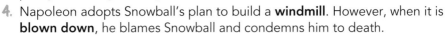

1. **Snowball** is **driven from** the farm; **Napoleon** behaves like a **tyrant**.
2. Sunday debates are **abolished** and the first commandment is **broken**.
3. Napoleon, protected by his **dogs**, changes policy, including **trading** with other farms.
4. Napoleon adopts Snowball's plan to build a **windmill**. However, when it is **blown down**, he blames Snowball and condemns him to death.
5. The animals **work harder** and get **little food**: things are much as they used to be in Jones's time.

What happens in Chapter 5?

- Mollie is lured away from the farm with sugar by a human.
- Snowball and Napoleon continue to disagree, especially over the windmill.
- Napoleon's dogs attack Snowball, who flees for his life. Squealer labels him **'no better than a criminal'**.
- Napoleon abolishes Sunday debates as his first move in taking control.
- Squealer, in charge of **propaganda**, says Napoleon is making a great sacrifice by taking responsibility for everything.
- The windmill will be built – but Squealer now says it was Napoleon's idea.

What happens in Chapter 6?

- Life worsens: the animals work 60 hours a week. Boxer works hardest, now starting work **'three-quarters of an hour earlier'** than anyone else.
- The construction of the windmill has problems and the harvest is poorer.
- Napoleon says he will trade with neighbouring farms, and the pigs break a commandment by sleeping in beds. They change the wording on the barn.
- When a storm destroys the windmill, Napoleon claims it was sabotaged and says **'I pronounce the death sentence upon Snowball'**. The animals must continue to work hard to rebuild the windmill.

Five key quotations

1. Squealer convinces the animals to accept their lot: **'Surely, comrades, you do not want Jones back?'** (Chapter 5)

2. Boxer has a simple attitude to what is happening: **'I will work harder'** and shows unquestioning loyalty: **'Napoleon is always right'** (Chapter 6)

3. The work on the windmill is exhausting: **'it was a slow, laborious process'** (Chapter 6)

4. Life becomes as bad as it used to be: **'All that year the animals worked like slaves.'** (Chapter 6)

5. The fourth commandment is changed: **'No animal shall sleep in a bed *with sheets*'** (Chapter 6)

Note it!

Notice how Squealer is always used by Napoleon to persuade the animals that all is well and that Napoleon is looking out for their best interests. The dogs provide the physical threat; Squealer offers what always seem to be convincing explanations.

Exam focus

How can I write about the changes at Animal Farm? AO1

You can show how Napoleon takes away the animals' freedoms and begins to change the course of the revolution.

Once Snowball has been driven out, Napoleon becomes like a dictator. He changes the animals' memories of events and even begins to alter the commandments: 'No animal shall sleep in a bed with sheets.' Orwell expects the reader to understand the significance, although the animals accept the alteration since Squealer justifies it. Ironically, life becomes as grim as it was when Mr Jones was still in charge.

- Topic sentence introduces the point
- Point is explained further
- Quotation effectively embedded
- Point is developed

Now you try!

Finish this paragraph about how even in such taxing times Boxer continues to do more than any other character to make Animal Farm a success. Use one of the quotations from the list.

Boxer ignores the hardships, doing all the pigs ask of him, and repeating his simple mantra ....

My progress Needs more work ☐ Getting there ☐ Sorted! ☐

PLOT AND STRUCTURE Chapters 7 and 8

Five key things about Chapters 7 and 8

In Chapters 7 and 8, conditions for the animals deteriorate still further and Napoleon is outwitted by the humans.

1. The animals face **starvation**, working harder but eating less than in Jones's time.
2. There is a **rebellion** on the farm, which is violently crushed.
3. Just as occurred in **Russia**, the **aims of the revolution** have been **corrupted**. Napoleon now uses **terror** to maintain control.
4. Napoleon tries to **trade** with the humans but is outwitted. The windmill is **rebuilt** but then **destroyed** by Frederick.
5. The pigs continue to **change** the Seven Commandments.

What happens in Chapter 7?

- When Napoleon decides to sell the hens' eggs, the hens rebel, but they are starved into submission.

- Everything that goes wrong is blamed on Snowball, who Squealer says was always in league with Jones. The animals feel Snowball is **'menacing them'**.

- Animals are executed after admitting they schemed with Snowball, whose reputation worsens as history is changed. This concerns Boxer.

- The singing of 'Beasts of England' is forbidden as the revolution is over.

What happens in Chapter 8?

- Two more commandments are changed so that it becomes acceptable to kill animals if there is a good cause (pigs, hens, a goose and a sheep are executed), and alcohol can be drunk, if not to excess.

- Napoleon becomes further isolated from the animals but is still praised for everything that goes well – he awards himself new honours.

- Napoleon tries to play Frederick and Pilkington off against each other, but is outwitted.

- The windmill is totally destroyed by Frederick's men. The animals drive them off in the Battle of the Windmill, but there is nothing at all left to show for their efforts: it is **'as though the windmill had never been'**.

Five key quotations

1. Napoleon is talked about with great respect: **'our Leader, Comrade Napoleon'** (Chapter 8)

2. The reign of terror is maintained with violence: **'the dogs promptly tore their throats out'** (Chapter 7)

3. Sorrow has replaced hope: **'As Clover looked down the hillside her eyes filled with tears.'** (Chapter 7)

4. The sixth commandment is changed: **'No animal shall kill any other animal *without cause.*'** (Chapter 7)

5. The fifth commandment is changed: **'No animal shall drink alcohol *to excess.*'** (Chapter 8)

Note it!

Notice how important Squealer is to Napoleon – how he persuades the animals that all is well and Napoleon can do no wrong. Squealer seems always to be positive, but notice the **'ugly look'** he gives Boxer in Chapter 7 when Boxer contradicts him.

Exam focus

How can I write about the animals' lives worsening? (A01)

You can explore the actions of Napoleon, which cause such terror and hardship.

Napoleon makes the lives of the animals a misery and their suffering is intended to make the reader empathise with them. They have less food because of his mismanagement and they have to work harder. When they have built the windmill for the second time, it is not defended and Frederick's men blow it up so it must be rebuilt again. Worst of all, his dogs bring a reign of terror: 'the dogs promptly tore their throats out'.

Topic sentence introduces the point

Supporting detail to explain point

Development supported by quotation

Now you try!

Finish this paragraph to show how Napoleon also uses Squealer's propaganda to help cement his control. Use one of the quotations from the list.

Squealer skips around saying only positive things about Napoleon, so he is always referred to with respect as ....

My progress   Needs more work ☐   Getting there ☐   Sorted! ☐   13

Five key things about Chapters 9 and 10

In Chapters 9 and 10, life for most on Animal Farm is worse than it ever was. The pigs, meanwhile, become indistinguishable from humans.

1. The pigs have **complete control** – the other animals are simply **oppressed**.
2. The pigs lead a life of **luxury** and are **anthropomorphic** in their **vices**.
3. Old Major's hopes turn out to be mere dreams. The **revolution** has **failed**.
4. **Boxer** is sold for meat and we **empathise** over his dreadful end.
5. The pigs dine with the humans and Animal Farm is symbolically renamed **Manor Farm**.

What happens in Chapter 9?

- The animals are starving as rations have been reduced still further, though the pigs do not suffer.
- Boxer will not rest. Even with a damaged hoof, he **'refused to take even a day off work'**.
- The young pigs are kept separate from the other animals, and all pigs have to be treated with respect.
- Animal Farm is declared a Republic and Napoleon is President.
- Boxer can work no more and the slaughter-house man takes him away: the pigs buy whisky with the money they get for him.

What happens in Chapter 10?

- With the passing years, the younger animals do not understand Animalism or remember Snowball and Boxer.
- The windmill has been rebuilt and another is being constructed; the farm is richer but the animals have not benefited.

- The Seven Commandments are replaced by a single slogan, the ultimate irony: **'All animals are equal but some animals are more equal than others'**.
- The pigs walk on their hind legs and live the life of humans. They carry whips.
- The pigs hold a banquet for neighbouring farmers: the other animals cannot distinguish between the faces of the humans and those of the pigs.

Five key quotations

1. Moses, who represents religion, returns with a fantasy of a wonderful eternity to come: **'Sugarcandy Mountain, that happy country where we poor animals shall rest for ever from our labours'** (Chapter 9)

2. Ironically, the animals still think they have a better life: **'And yet the animals never gave up hope.'** (Chapter 10)

3. The sheep's bleating supports the changes in the pigs: **'Four legs good, two legs better!'** (Chapter 10)

4. The commandments are replaced by one **oxymoron**: **'All animals are equal but some animals are more equal than others'** (Chapter 10)

5. The animals see that pigs and humans are just the same: **'it was impossible to say which was which'** (Chapter 10)

Note it!

Benjamin, the cynic, is proved to have been correct. Notice how many details at the end demonstrate that the uprising has been a failure and Old Major's hopes were no more than dreams.

Exam focus

How can I write about the novel's effective conclusion?

You can explore how the revolution has turned full circle.

By the end of the novel, Napoleon is no better than Jones and the animals are exploited more than they ever were before.	Topic sentence introduces the point
Napoleon is friends with the humans – indeed, he looks just like them – and Orwell	Point is developed
proves that *all hope brought by the revolution has died because there is no equality* with the farm's final	Explanation of quotation
slogan: 'All animals are equal but some animals are more equal than others.'	Quotation effectively embedded

Now you try!

Finish this paragraph to show what Napoleon has become by the end of the novel. Use one of the quotations from the list.

By the end, Napoleon and the pigs have become just like the humans ....

PLOT AND STRUCTURE Form and structure

Three key things about form and structure

Animal Farm is written like a traditional story for **children**.

1. It has **anthropomorphic** characters and a **simple storyline**.
2. It is Orwell's **satire** on the **Russian Revolution** and an **allegory** of events in Russian history.
3. The **plot** is circular, showing no improvement is made – so Benjamin, the cynic, was right all along.

How is the satire presented?

- Animals represent historical figures or stereotypes. For example, Napoleon's character is based on Stalin and Boxer represents the ordinary people.
- Symbols are used to simplify the story, so the farm is Russia and the Battle of the Windmill represents the German invasion of Russia.
- **Ironic** humour highlights what goes wrong for the animals, for example when the pigs develop each of the faults for which the humans were criticised.

What use is made of the simple storyline?

- The simple farmyard setting makes the brutality of the pigs' regime more unexpected and disturbing.
- In stories for children, good usually triumphs over evil. In *Animal Farm*, the opposite happens.
- By using simple characters and a naïve tone, Orwell is able to make complex political points effectively.

How does the story develop?

- The pigs gradually take complete control, as shown by the altering of the Seven Commandments.
- Following a positive start after the revolution, life becomes increasingly hard for the animals and more luxurious for the pigs.
- By the end, Napoleon has become just as oppressive as Jones. He carries a whip and, **symbolically**, the pigs have grown to look exactly like the humans.

16

Five key quotations

1. *Animal Farm* is different from a traditional children's story: **'the dogs had tasted blood, and ... appeared to go quite mad'** (Chapter 7)
2. There is a circular nature to what happens: **'the farm had grown richer without making the animals themselves any richer'** (Chapter 10)
3. The oppression is as bad as in Jones's time: **'The pigs ... all carried whips in their trotters'** (Chapter 10)
4. Considering the ending, what Old Major said was ironic: **'all the evil ... springs from the tyranny of human beings'** (Chapter 1)
5. The animals see that pigs and humans are just the same, as Pilkington explains: **'Between pigs and human beings there were not ... any clash of interests whatever.'** (Chapter 10)

Note it!

Notice how Squealer can twist reality so that the animals accept conditions that become worse and worse for them, and how he justifies the improvements for the pigs.

Exam focus

How can I explore Orwell's use of satire?

You can write about how Orwell exposes how the animals are fooled by the pigs.

As occurred in the Russian Revolution, the animals – who represent the Russian people – think they can achieve a better standard of living. However, by the end we see that 'the farm had grown richer without making the animals any richer'. This is because they are easily deceived and Squealer can convince them of whatever the state (in this case the pigs) wishes.	Topic sentence introduces the point
	Link shows the satire
	Quotation effectively embedded
	Development of the point being made

Now you try!

Finish this paragraph to show how the circular plot leaves the animals treated as badly as ever they were. Use one of the quotations from the list.

Old Major's speech is ironic, because by the end of the novel the oppression is as bad as in Jones's time ....

1. Look at this ideas map about how nothing changes for the better in *Animal Farm*. Is there anything else you could add?

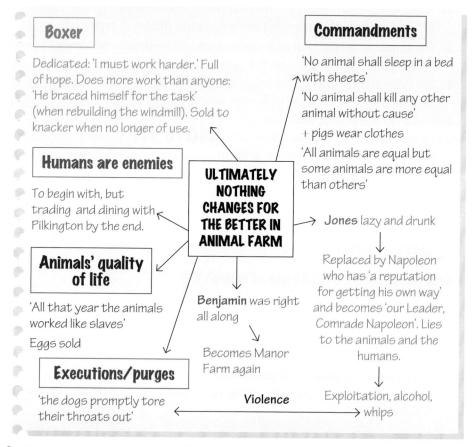

Boxer

Dedicated: 'I must work harder.' Full of hope. Does more work than anyone: 'He braced himself for the task' (when rebuilding the windmill). Sold to knacker when no longer of use.

Humans are enemies

To begin with, but trading and dining with Pilkington by the end.

Animals' quality of life

'All that year the animals worked like slaves'

Eggs sold

Executions/purges

'the dogs promptly tore their throats out'

ULTIMATELY NOTHING CHANGES FOR THE BETTER IN ANIMAL FARM

Commandments

'No animal shall sleep in a bed with sheets'

'No animal shall kill any other animal without cause'

+ pigs wear clothes

'All animals are equal but some animals are more equal than others'

Jones lazy and drunk

Replaced by Napoleon who has 'a reputation for getting his own way' and becomes 'our Leader, Comrade Napoleon'. Lies to the animals and the humans.

Exploitation, alcohol, whips

Violence

Benjamin was right all along

Becomes Manor Farm again

2. Create your own ideas map for another aspect of the plot.

Quick quiz

Answer these quick questions about plot and structure.

1. Who are the leaders of the pigs?
2. Who leads the Sunday debates?
3. What do the pigs decide 'would form an unalterable law'?
4. Who were the most 'faithful disciples' of the revolution?

5. Which men try to take back the farm?

6. What does Squealer say regularly to suggest that life could be worse?

7. What is the first thing Napoleon does when he takes control?

8. According to Squealer, who is 'no better than a criminal'?

9. Who gets up earliest for work in the morning?

10. Who is blamed for the destruction of the first windmill?

11. What happens when Napoleon decides to sell the hens' eggs?

12. Why does Squealer 'cast a very ugly look at Boxer'?

13. Who destroys the second windmill?

14. How do the pigs celebrate victory in the Battle of the Windmill?

15. Boxer manages to continue to work despite what injury?

16. Who is the first pig seen walking on his hind legs?

17. What do the pigs do with the money they get for Boxer?

18. What is the name of the happy land that Moses says exists?

19. In what ways are the pigs anthropomorphic?

20. In what way is the plot of *Animal Farm* circular?

Power paragraphs

Write **a paragraph** in response to **each of these questions**. For each, try to **use one quotation** you have learned from this section.

1. How does Orwell use the changing of the Seven Commandments to convey his message that nothing ever seems to improve on the farm?

2. Napoleon invites the neighbouring farmers to dine at the end: in what ways is he like them?

Exam practice

Re-read the final paragraph of *Animal Farm* from 'Twelve voices were shouting in anger ...' to '... it was impossible to say which was which'. Why is it important in the novel as a whole?

Write **two paragraphs** explaining your ideas.

You should comment on:

● what happens in the paragraph at the end of the novel

● why this is important after what has happened in the story.

SETTING AND CONTEXT
Communism and totalitarianism

Five key things about Communism and totalitarianism

1. Russian **Communism** grew from the teachings of Karl Marx (represented by Old Major), who wanted a better system than **capitalism**.

2. In the new **Soviet Union**, after the **Russian Revolution of 1917**, all property, wealth and work were meant to be divided **equally** between all the people.

3. This Communism was established by **Lenin** and **Trotsky**, but after Lenin's death **Stalin** took over and Trotsky fled.

4. Stalin then corrupted Communism, developing a **totalitarian** state in which an all-powerful **dictator** imposes their absolute will.

5. In such a state, the dictator, surrounded by a ruling elite, uses **violence** and **propaganda** to control the working class, or **proletariat**.

How does Animal Farm mirror Communist ideals?

- Animalism is a simplified form of Communism. It replaces the corrupt capitalism of Animal Farm which exploited the animals.
- The Seven Commandments set out the rules that make everyone equal.
- After the revolution, at first life on the farm improves.
- Snowball sets out grand improvements, to benefit all in the future: '**the animals would only need to work three days a week**'.

In what ways does Animal Farm become a dictatorial state?

- Napoleon corrupts Old Major's dream of equality, imposing an authoritarian regime. He uses lies, propaganda and terror to maintain his position.
- The pigs – the elite – have the best of everything and carry whips: they live in the house and eat and drink well while the other animals starve.
- The use of 'comrade' – implying equality – is banned, and the representations of Animalism are removed from the flag.
- Napoleon proudly explains to his neighbours how the animals are exploited.
- Animal Farm is as corrupt as neighbouring farms. The pigs feast while the hungry animals watch through the window.

Five key quotations

1. Old Major sums up Animalism (Communism): **'All animals are equal.'** (Chapter 1)

2. He believes in a fairer system: **'Only get rid of Man, and the produce of our labour would be our own.'** (Chapter 1)

3. The revolution is totally undermined: **'the farm had grown richer without making the animals themselves any richer'** (Chapter 10)

4. Napoleon's dictatorial state is brutal: **'the air was heavy with the smell of blood'** (Chapter 7)

5. Pilkington applauds the new state for its unfairness: **'the lower animals on Animal Farm did more work and received less food than any animals in the country'** (Chapter 10)

Note it!

Totalitarianism – a form of absolute rule – is also closely connected to fascism, as practised by leaders like Hitler and Mussolini. Consider any parallels drawn with Napoleon and these two dictators by Orwell.

Exam focus

How can I apply ideas about Communism to the characters? AO2

You can write about how Orwell uses characters like Old Major and Napoleon to represent key political ideas.

Describing his dream, Old Major sets out a vision of a fairer future, just as Karl Marx explained his hopes and communist ideals. When Old Major says 'All animals are equal', he is establishing a philosophy of hope. However, Orwell goes on to show how Napoleon corrupts Animalism and turns the farm into a dictatorial state.

> Topic sentence introduces the point

> Embedded quotation extends the idea

> Further development of the idea

Now you try!

Finish this paragraph to show how Napoleon makes the farm a totalitarian state. Use one of the quotations from the list.

Under Napoleon's authoritarian leadership, the animals are treated cruelly and oppressively, so that the very air of the farm is . . . .

My progress   Needs more work ☐   Getting there ☐   Sorted! ☐   21

Five key things about the Russian Revolution

1. After the Russian Revolution in **1917**, when the **ruling Tsar** was driven out, a Communist state was formed.
2. The state was based on equality and the teachings of **Karl Marx**, and was led by **Trotsky** and **Lenin**.
3. When Lenin died, **Stalin** seized control of what had become the Soviet Union.
4. Stalin's policies brought **starvation**. He was a **tyrant** who took complete control, **purging** his enemies: from 1934 to 1937, seven million of his people disappeared.
5. The Soviet Union was an **ally** of the **USA** and **Great Britain** during the Second World War, but then the Cold War began and it became isolated again.

How does the story of Animal Farm work as a satire?

- Orwell devised *Animal Farm* as 'a **satire** on the Russian Revolution' through which he could portray how all dictators work.
- He wanted to show the Russian Revolution as corrupt and socialism as a force for good.
- Writing the story in a simple form meant that its message could be easily understood by all.

What are the connections to key figures of the revolution?

- Old Major is like Karl Marx – and Animalism is like Communism.
- Snowball is partly like Lenin, the first leader of the Soviet Union, and partly like Trotsky, who led the army to victory in the civil war.
- Napoleon, the cruel leader who becomes increasingly repressive, is like Stalin.
- Pilkington represents Churchill while Frederick represents Hitler – Stalin had dealings with both in the 1930s and 1940s.
- Boxer represents the working class or proletariat, Mr Jones is the Tsar, Squealer is the **propaganda** machine, Moses is the Russian Orthodox Church, the dogs are the secret police and Clover is one of the loyal followers.

Five key quotations

1. Like the Russian people, the animals are optimistic about change to begin with: **'it was truly their own food'** (Chapter 3)

2. The animals initially gain freedom after the revolution: **'All the animals capered with joy when they saw the whips going up in flames.'** (Chapter 2)

3. Napoleon (Stalin) has dealings with both Pilkington (Churchill) and Frederick (Hitler): **'By seeming to be friendly with Pilkington he had forced Frederick to raise his price'** (Chapter 8)

4. Equality is eroded, so 'All animals are equal' changes: **'All animals are equal but some animals are more equal than others'** (Chapter 10)

5. By the end, the pigs are just like humans: **'it was impossible to say which was which'** (Chapter 10)

Note it!

Notice how religion (represented by Moses) has no role on Animal Farm until later, when life is grim, and it is allowed back to give hope, or the fantasy, of something better after death.

Exam focus

How can I link the Russian Revolution to the novel? **AO3**

When writing about characters or themes, the Russian Revolution can underpin your ideas.

When Jones is driven out, the animals think they have a wonderful future ahead of them, but as with the Russian Revolution the initial idealism is destroyed. Napoleon and the pigs corrupt Old Major's dream of equality, so that by the end when they dine with the humans 'it was impossible to say which was which'. The new regime has become just like the old regime of Mr Jones.

Topic sentence makes reference to content

Successfully embedded quotation

Effective summary

Now you try!

Finish this paragraph about how the animals feel when they drive out Mr Jones. Use one of the quotations from the list.

When Jones is driven out, the animals think their lives will be better and, indeed, at first ....

Three key things about the farm

1. All the **action** is set on the farm, part of Orwell's 'simple approach'.
2. The farm represents **Russia**, which later became the **Soviet Union**.
3. It becomes **Animal Farm** after the revolution, but reverts to its original name of **Manor Farm** when Napoleon is in charge at the end.

How realistic is the farm?

- Although the animals are **anthropomorphic** – like humans – activities on the farm are quite normal: the animals are fed, cows are milked and crops are grown.
- There are recognisable animal traits: for example, pigs are intelligent, and dogs can be trained and are aggressive.
- The sheep are passive and easily controlled, so when they learn their maxim (**'Four legs good, two legs bad'**) they bleat it **'for hours on end, never growing tired of it'**.

What are the most important places on the farm?

- The farmhouse is set apart: it is initially where Jones lives and later where the pigs establish themselves. The animals **'were frightened to go inside'**.
- The barn is where Old Major tells of his dream, where meetings are held and where Napoleon first unleashes his dogs. The Seven Commandments are painted on its end wall.
- Battles take place near the cowshed and then the windmill, which represents the dream of a better life, though the generation of wind power just makes money for the pigs.

Three quotations about the farm

1. Old Major's view of farm life: **'The life of an animal is misery and slavery'** (Chapter 1)
2. Even when the purges begin, the animals remain positive about their land: **'it was their own farm, every inch of it their own property'** (Chapter 7)
3. By the end: **'the lower animals on Animal Farm did more work and received less food than any animals in the country'** (Chapter 10)

Quick quiz

1. Who ruled Russia before the revolution?
2. What did Karl Marx think Communism was better than?
3. What is the equivalent of Communism on the farm?
4. Which character represents Stalin?
5. What was Russia renamed after the revolution?
6. Where are the Seven Commandments painted?
7. What did Trotsky do in the Russian Revolution?
8. Which quotation shows what Old Major thinks about the animals' life before the revolution?
9. Where do the two battles take place on the farm?
10. Which quotation shows that there is no equality at the end of the novel?

Power paragraphs

Write **two paragraphs** explaining the animals' feelings about the farm: a) immediately after the revolution and b) at the end, when the pigs are in total control.

Five key things about Old Major

Old Major is important because his speech presents the ideology on which the revolution is based, but his words sound **ironic** after the pigs take control.

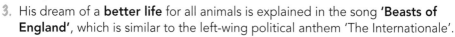

1. Just as Karl Marx set out the theory of **Communism**, so Old Major devises **Animalism**.
2. He is twelve years old and considered **wise**, so everyone comes to listen.
3. His dream of a **better life** for all animals is explained in the song **'Beasts of England'**, which is similar to the left-wing political anthem 'The Internationale'.
4. He views all **humans** as the enemy of animals.
5. His teaching is finally **overturned** by the pigs, who exhibit all the human vices he warns against. Even his skull, a **symbol** of his teaching, is removed from beneath the flagpole and buried.

What does Old Major think of humans?

- Humans are responsible for everything that is wrong in the animals' lives.
- For their own purposes, humans use animals' labour, take what animals produce and slaughter them.
- Man only cares about himself, but **'Tyrant Man shall be o'erthrown'**.

How can the animals' lives change?

- They can rebel and then be free and well fed.
- They will have a glorious future, including **'Riches more than mind can picture'**.

How do Old Major's words become ironic?

- Old Major warns the animals about false arguments: they believe Squealer.
- He says animals have no common interests with Man: Napoleon trades with the neighbouring farmers. He says man is the only enemy and all animals are friends: Pilkington dines with Napoleon and animals are executed.
- He warns that no animal must ever **'tyrannize over his own kind'**: purges take place and the pigs carry whips.
- He dreams of **'the golden future time'**: things worsen by the end of the novel.

Five key quotations

1. Old Major identifies what he sees as the problem: **'Man is the only real enemy we have.'** (Chapter 1)

2. He is wrong in his vision of the future: **'Remove Man from the scene, and the root cause of hunger and overwork is abolished for ever.'** (Chapter 1)

3. Equally ironically, he thinks that without a change, even Boxer will be sold: **'Jones will sell you to the knacker'** (Chapter 1)

4. He has a clear vision: **'All men are enemies. All animals are comrades.'** (Chapter 1)

5. He devises Animalism: **'we are all brothers'** (Chapter 1)

Note it!

Look through Old Major's speech and notice how he convinces the animals of his ideas, by giving examples and using persuasive phrasing, including rhetorical questions.

Exam focus

How can I show the importance of Old Major's speech? AO1 AO2

You can write about how his ideas are at first adopted but then distorted as the plot unfolds.

> At the beginning of the novel, the animals find Old Major's words inspiring, but they never achieve the benefits he expects. He criticises Man: 'Remove Man from the scene, and the root cause of hunger and overwork is abolished for ever' but Orwell shows that the root of the animals' problems is actually greed. This is shown through the pigs, who only pretend to follow Old Major's ideas and instead adopt men's vices, becoming just as greedy and tyrannical as Farmer Jones ever was.

Topic sentence introduces the point

Point is further explained

Quotation embedded to support point

Further development of point

Now you try!

Finish this paragraph to show how Orwell uses irony in Old Major's speech. Use one of the quotations from the list.

The irony of the example Old Major gives, of Farmer Jones selling even Boxer . . . .

Five key things about Snowball

Snowball is a leader of the revolution but is later driven out by Napoleon and Squealer, who ensure his reputation is ruined.

1. After the revolution, he cares for the animals, promotes their **education**, and is **popular**.
2. He plans the **windmill** to bring future **prosperity** and leads bravely in the Battle of the Cowshed.
3. He accepts that the pigs should have apples and milk, though he **generally disagrees** with Napoleon.
4. He is suddenly **attacked** by the dogs and **flees**, and Napoleon takes control.
5. In Snowball's absence, he is **blamed** for everything that goes wrong from that point on, and Squealer convinces the animals he is a **threat** to the farm.

What are Snowball's qualities?

- He has characteristics of Trotsky and Lenin, leaders in the Russian Revolution and supporters of the Communist ideal. He paints the Seven Commandments on the barn and changes the farm's name.
- His name is **symbolic**, suggesting purity, although like a snowball he is effective at first, but will crumble or melt later.
- He establishes classes for the animals, showing his concern for their welfare: **'He was indefatigable at this.'**
- His intelligence is obvious, in designing the windmill and organising the defence in the Battle of the Cowshed.

To what extent is Snowball different from Napoleon?

- He sets up Animal Committees, allowing the animals to offer their opinions.
- He believes in democracy (using meetings to put forward his ideas), while **'Napoleon took no interest in Snowball's committees.'**
- Snowball uses military strategy, based on Julius Caesar's campaigns for the battle, and leads the fighting, being awarded **'Animal Hero, First Class'**.
- His agreeing with Napoleon that the pigs should have milk and apples suggests that Snowball is not perfect.
- He can be ruthless, having no sympathy for the men injured in the battle.

Five key quotations

1. Snowball has a lively, appealing personality: **'a more vivacious pig than Napoleon, quicker in speech and more inventive'** (Chapter 2)

2. He is not thought to be as serious as Napoleon: **'was not considered to have the same depth of character'** (Chapter 2)

3. Snowball simplifies things for the animals: **'Four legs good, two legs bad.'** (Chapter 3)

4. He is brave in battle: **'Snowball flung his fifteen stone against Jones's legs'** (Chapter 4)

5. He can be ruthless: **'The only good human being is a dead one.'** (Chapter 4)

Note it!

Notice all the things that are said about Snowball after he is driven out: what he is blamed for and how his reputation is destroyed. Note in particular the way Squealer undermines the memory of Snowball, describing him as **'a dangerous character and a bad influence'**.

Exam focus

How can I write about Snowball?

You can write about how Orwell describes Snowball, his actions, what these suggest about him and what others say of him.

Compared to Napoleon, Orwell shows Snowball is a positive influence on the animals' life after the revolution, though he is not perfect. He sets up committees and helps the animals understand Animalism: 'Four legs good, two legs bad.' However, he seems to collude with Napoleon when the pigs take the milk and apples, and seems heartless when humans are injured, which contrasts with Boxer's feelings.	Topic sentence introduces the point
	Further explanation of the point
	Quotation effectively embedded
	Development of point made by quotation

Now you try!

Finish this paragraph to show how Snowball leads the animals. Use one of the quotations from the list.

Orwell shows Snowball to have natural leadership qualities both in his planning before the battle and in his fearless actions ....

CHARACTERS Napoleon

Five key things about Napoleon

Napoleon represents Stalin, who established an authoritarian regime after the Russian Revolution.

1. His name reminds us of **Napoleon Bonaparte**, a revolutionary who became Emperor of France (1804).
2. He **controls** the animals' food and trains the puppies who expel Snowball.
3. To transform the farm into a totalitarian state, he uses **propaganda**, **purges** and **cruelty**.
4. He is **undemocratic** and becomes a deceitful tyrant.
5. By the end, he has taken Jones's place and **betrayed** the revolutionary ideals.

How does Napoleon gain total power?

- Napoleon uses his bodyguards – the dogs – to drive out Snowball.
- He gradually gains total control: undermining democracy and changing rules.
- Squealer's propaganda makes Napoleon seem faultless (even when plans go wrong, e.g. when the windmill collapses) and blames Snowball for everything.
- The purge – when animals confess to things they have not done – is used to terrify every animal into submission: **'They were shaken'**.
- Details of events are changed, to make Napoleon seem heroic.

What is especially evil about Napoleon?

- By betraying Animalism, he seems worse than Jones.
- He breaks and alters the commandments.
- Animals are slaughtered on his orders and Boxer is sold to the knacker.
- He lies throughout and gradually distances himself from the animals, e.g. when he moves into the farmhouse, taking everything for himself.

How is Napoleon deceitful?

- He claims to have designed the windmill and re-writes the farm's history.
- He makes separate deals with Pilkington and Frederick for the farm's timber.
- Napoleon is said to be responsible for victory at the Battle of the Cowshed.

30

Five key quotations

1. Orwell's first description of Napoleon sums him up: 'a large, rather fierce-looking Berkshire boar ... not much of a talker, but with a reputation for getting his own way' (Chapter 2)
2. He is undemocratic from the start: '**Never mind the milk, comrades**' (Chapter 2)
3. He rules through terror: '**the dogs sitting round Napoleon let out deep, menacing growls**' (Chapter 5)
4. Squealer makes claims for him: '**The windmill was ... Napoleon's own creation.**' (Chapter 5)
5. He betrays the revolution, telling Pilkington: '**Their sole wish ... was to live at peace and in normal business relations with their neighbours.**' (Chapter 10)

Note it!

Notice how all the aims of the revolution are steadily undermined by Napoleon; how what really happened is reimagined, and it is made to seem a logical progression when he appears in clothes, carries a whip and entertains humans.

Exam focus

How can I summarise Napoleon's tyranny? (AO1)

You can write about how Orwell shows how Napoleon changes the farm, so it moves away from its Communist roots.

Like Stalin, Napoleon first uses terror to seize control, then lies and propaganda to maintain it. From the start, he is fierce and Orwell tells us that he has 'a reputation for getting his own way', which perhaps suggests his deviousness and single-mindedness as well as his selfishness. As he becomes more human, he changes the Seven Commandments to suit himself, even executing pigs to remove any opposition.

| Topic sentence introduces the point |
| Appropriate embedded quotation |
| Explanation of the quotation |
| Further development |

Now you try!

Finish this paragraph to show how Napoleon deceives the other animals. Use one of the quotations from the list.

Although Napoleon does fight at the Battle of the Windmill, he deceives the animals with other claims about what he has done ....

My progress Needs more work ☐ Getting there ☐ Sorted! ☐ **31**

CHARACTERS Squealer

Five key things about Squealer

Squealer is the regime's **propagandist**, who aims to convince everyone that Napoleon is always right.

1. He makes the animals believe that all is well and Napoleon is ensuring their **wellbeing**.
2. He uses **persuasive rhetoric** to change their memories and introduces **false facts** to prove life has improved.
3. He is **devious** and **evil** in his support of Napoleon.
4. He is actually a **coward**, who is absent when the farm is being defended and has **dogs** around him for protection at other times.
5. He gains in importance and **weight**, indicating that Napoleon **rewards** him for his **loyalty**.

What methods does Squealer use to persuade the animals?

- His mantra is that all Napoleon's actions are to prevent the return of Jones.
- He is described as **'sly'** and challenges any possible dissent, e.g. asking if there is any written proof for what the animals think they remember.
- He is smoothly persuasive and eloquent, using rhetorical questions, e.g. **'Surely you remember *that*, comrades?'**.
- He purposely uses words the animals do not understand, like **'files'** and **'memoranda'**. Impressive language that misleads is a feature of propaganda.
- Often, he uses an emotive approach when describing Napoleon, even bursting into tears when describing Napoleon's qualities.

How is Squealer a sinister character?

- He uses his ability to justify even the worst incidents, such as the purges.
- He presents himself as the voice of reason but is actually threatening: **'his little eyes darted suspicious glances from side to side'**.
- He changes 'truth' – and trains the sheep to chant **'Four legs good, two legs better'** to help enforce his message.
- His role is to ensure that there is no opposition to Napoleon, e.g. he even gives Boxer an **'ugly look'** when he speaks in favour of Snowball.

Five key quotations

1. He is a 'brilliant talker': 'he could turn black into white' (Chapter 2)
2. He repeats the same threat: 'Surely, comrades, you do not want Jones back?' (Chapter 5)
3. He uses an emotive approach: 'Squealer would talk with the tears running down his cheeks of Napoleon's wisdom' (Chapter 8)
4. He is a consummate liar: 'he had no difficulty in proving to the other animals that they were *not* in reality short of food' (Chapter 9)
5. He grows fat thanks to the animals' labours: 'Squealer was so fat that he could with difficulty see out of his eyes.' (Chapter 10)

Note it!

Although Squealer speaks so positively, notice how Orwell shows, e.g. in references to his glances and his eyes, that he feels other emotions such as distrust, and that he is insecure in his role because he is guarded by dogs.

Exam focus

How can I write about how Squealer changes? AO1

You can write about the physical changes and how his less pleasant characteristics are revealed.

Squealer changes significantly as the story develops. At first, he skips around, radiating energy as he talks but, by the end, 'Squealer was so fat that he could with difficulty see out of his eyes' and he slows down. Similarly, his bright cheeriness is later shown to mask evil underneath, as we are expected to recognise he is lying. He becomes a real threat to anyone who does not seem to be supporting Napoleon totally – even Boxer.	Topic sentence introduces the point
	Supported by quotation
	Expands point with wider reference
	Point developed further

Now you try!

Finish this paragraph to show how Squealer convinces the animals that Napoleon acts in their interests. Use one of the quotations from the list.

Orwell reveals how devious Squealer is, as he uses emotive phrases to persuade the animals ....

My progress   Needs more work   Getting there   Sorted!   33

Five key things about Boxer

Boxer is the novel's tragic hero, dedicated to the revolution but betrayed by Napoleon at the end.

1. Boxer, the carthorse, represents the **working classes**, decent, labouring harder than others and **believing** what he is told.
2. Boxer's **strength** and **long hours** of work make Animal Farm a **success**.
3. He shows **integrity** by defending Snowball and **compassion** when he thinks he has killed the stable-lad.
4. When no longer useful, he is **sold** to the knacker: which is **ironic** because this is what Old Major said Jones would do with him.
5. We are **sympathetic** to Boxer because of his honesty, decency and commitment, and because he is **tricked** by the pigs.

Why is Boxer important to the farm?

- Boxer is largely responsible for the heavy work on the farm, and the building of the windmills.
- With Snowball, he is at the forefront in the Battle of the Cowshed (awarded **'Animal Hero, First Class'**) and also in the Battle of the Windmill.

How does Orwell generate sympathy for Boxer?

- Boxer never complains.
- He may lack intelligence – he cannot remember beyond the letter D – but compensates for this with his hard work and compassion.
- Although he fights for the farm, he does not wish to hurt anyone and spares the dogs when they attack him.
- After the windmill is blown up, he rises an hour earlier to help rebuild it. He and Clover are the **'most faithful disciples'** of the revolution.
- He works on, even with a split hoof. When he can no longer contribute, he is not given retirement, but is taken for horsemeat, and is too weak to break out of the knacker's van. The final view of him, with his nose at the van window, is pitiful.

Five key quotations

1. In the Battle of the Cowshed, Boxer is upset to have caused harm: 'Who will believe that I did not do this on purpose?' (Chapter 4)
2. Boxer has two mantras: 'I will work harder' and 'Napoleon is always right' (Chapter 6)
3. Boxer has blind faith in the pigs: 'It must be due to some fault in ourselves.' (Chapter 7)
4. Ironically, Old Major tells him: 'Boxer, the very day that those great muscles of yours lose their power, Jones will sell you to the knacker' (Chapter 1)
5. The emotive moment when Boxer is taken away: 'Boxer's face, with the white stripe down his nose, appeared at the small window at the back of the van' (Chapter 9)

Note it!

Notice how our sympathy is elicited when Boxer is taken by the knacker, and also what the incident tells us about the callousness of the pigs.

Exam focus

What is Boxer's importance in the novel? AO1 AO3

You can write about what he contributes to the farm and how easily he is led by the pigs.

> Boxer represents the workers, and he dedicates himself to the success of Animal Farm. Not only does he commit to long hours and selfless labour, he never complains about the conditions or criticises the pigs. If something is wrong, he says: 'It must be due to some fault in ourselves.' Whatever happens, he maintains his faith in the pigs, which is a symbol of how the working classes are always manipulated by those in power.

Topic sentence introduces the point

Explanation of the point

Embedded quotation provides evidence

Widens point to show context

Now you try!

Finish this paragraph to show Boxer's essential goodness. Use one of the quotations from the list.

Boxer is dedicated to making the farm a success, but not at any cost because he does not want to hurt anyone ....

My progress   Needs more work ☐   Getting there ☐   Sorted! ☐

CHARACTERS Clover and Benjamin

Three key things about Clover

Like Benjamin, Clover is a friend of Boxer.

1. She is the **motherly mare** who also represents the **working classes**.
2. She is easily **exploited**, and does not act on her **doubts** about the pigs' decisions.
3. She is **desperate** to save Boxer when he is taken away, but fails.

How is Clover important to the story?

- She has our sympathy because she is so caring, e.g. protecting the ducklings.
- She is slightly more intelligent than Boxer (she learns the alphabet) and suspects that commandments are being changed, but can be convinced that this is not happening.
- After the executions and when the pigs are entertaining, Orwell changes **narrative viewpoint** and we are told Clover's thoughts. This helps us empathise both with her and the other animals: **'her eyes filled with tears'**.

Three key things about Benjamin

Benjamin the **donkey** has lived a long time, and is wise.

1. He is a **cynic**, doubting anything will improve and saying **cryptically**: 'Donkeys live a long time.'
2. He **refuses to comment** on the revolution. He fights in the Battle of the Cowshed but does not celebrate the revolution.
3. Benjamin **alerts the animals** when Boxer is taken away, but **cannot help him**.

What is Benjamin's function in the novel?

- He gives a long-term view of life, knowing conditions are unlikely to improve.
- He represents those who recognise evil but do nothing to fight against it: the good people in society who allow evil to triumph.
- Although he does not oppose the pigs, he is a sympathetic character because of his friendship with Boxer.

Five key quotations

1. Clover has relatively limited intelligence: **'Clover learnt the whole alphabet, but could not put words together.'** (Chapter 3)
2. Her motherliness is made clear after the executions: **'The animals huddled about Clover, not speaking.'** (Chapter 7)
3. Benjamin is old, wise and cantankerous: **'Benjamin was the oldest animal on the farm, and the worst tempered.'** (Chapter 1)
4. When Squealer is found with paint, having altered the commandments: **'Benjamin ... nodded his muzzle with a knowing air ... but would say nothing'** (Chapter 8)
5. Benjamin's pessimistic view of existence: **'hunger, hardship, and disappointment being, so he said, the unalterable law of life'** (Chapter 10)

Note it!

Notice how Benjamin is the one who usually understands what is actually happening on the farm – for instance, when Frederick is going to blow up the windmill.

Exam focus

How can I write about Orwell's use of Clover's viewpoint?

You can write about how the narrative viewpoint reveals Clover's thoughts after the executions and at the end of the novel.

By giving access to Clover's thoughts, Orwell encourages the reader to empathise with her – and with the animals. When they are 'huddled around Clover, not speaking', we understand that the animals go to her because she represents a comforting mother figure. Her eyes fill with tears, and we know she is instinctively lamenting the fact that their dreams have been dashed and that the farm animals are once again oppressed. The tragedy is made personal.

- Topic sentence introduces the point
- Quotation effectively embedded
- Explanation of quotation
- Further development and conclusion

Now you try!

Finish this paragraph to show Benjamin's role as a realist and cynic. Use one of the quotations from the list.

Orwell conveys the impression that the long-lived Benjamin knows exactly what is going on . . . .

My progress Needs more work ☐   Getting there ☐   Sorted! ☐   **37**

Three key things about the other animals

The other animals represent a range of characteristics.

1. The **pigs use the sheep** to **quell opposition**; the dogs **control** the animals.
2. Only the **hens oppose** the pigs.
3. Mollie, Moses and the cat **do nothing** to support the revolution.

What do the other animals represent?

- The sheep are easily led. They bleat **'Four legs good, two legs bad'**, to drown out opposition to Napoleon in meetings. Later, Squealer trains them to bleat **'Four legs good, two legs better'**.
- The dogs are the pigs' elite bodyguards, attacking any opposition and terrifying the other animals.
- The hens are workers who rebel, but Napoleon ruthlessly defeats them.
- Mollie, like the Russian elite, is self-centred: **'Will there still be sugar after the Rebellion?'**
- Moses represents orthodox religion – he flees but returns when the revolution fails.
- The cat is a scrounger, contributing nothing to the farm, but wanting the benefits.

Three key things about the humans

1. The humans are all **unattractive**, **corrupt** and work against Animal Farm.
2. They fear the revolution might **cause unrest** elsewhere.
3. They are **pleased** when the farm **reverts** to its former state.

Who are the most significant humans?

- Jones: like the Russian Tsar, he takes no care of those in his charge.
- Pilkington: a gentleman farmer, who does not look after Foxwood Farm, represents Churchill.
- Frederick: like Hitler, who had a pact with Stalin but then invaded Russia. He tricks Napoleon over the timber.
- Whymper: **'a sly-looking little man'**, who is the solicitor doing Napoleon's bidding and profiting from the animals' misery.

Five key quotations

1. The sheep bleat obediently: 'as usual, the sheep broke into "Four legs good, two legs bad!" and the momentary awkwardness was smoothed over' (Chapter 6)

2. The dogs are ruthlessly aggressive: '**the dogs promptly tore their throats out**' (Chapter 7)

3. Napoleon ends the hens' rebellion: 'He ... decreed that any animal giving as much as a grain of corn to a hen should be punished by death.' (Chapter 7)

4. Jones is shown as an uncaring farmer: '**too drunk to remember to shut the popholes**' (Chapter 1)

5. Pilkington says the pigs are just like humans: '**Their struggles and their difficulties were one.**' (Chapter 10)

Note it!

Notice how Orwell describes all the humans as evil – even the knacker's man who takes Boxer away. He is another '**sly-looking man**', this time '**in a low-crowned bowler hat**'.

Exam focus

How can I write about the significance of Pilkington and Frederick? (AO1)

You can focus on how they represent evil in humankind and later how the pigs resemble them.

Pilkington and Frederick, who represent Hitler and Churchill, are neighbouring farmers who are corrupt and initially try to undermine Animal Farm. Gradually, however, they realise that they can do business with the pigs in the same ways they dealt with Jones. Indeed, by the end, Pilkington goes so far as to say 'Their struggles and their difficulties were one', accepting Napoleon as his counterpart.

- Topic sentence introduces the point
- Develops point further
- Appropriate integrated quotation
- Draws conclusion from quotation

Now you try!

Finish this paragraph to explain how the sheep and dogs help the pigs. Use one of the quotations from the list.

Orwell demonstrates, through the ways in which the pigs use the sheep's bleating, how Napoleon manipulates the obedient animals ....

CHARACTERS Quick revision

1. Look at this ideas map about how Snowball is presented in the novel. Is there anything else you could add?

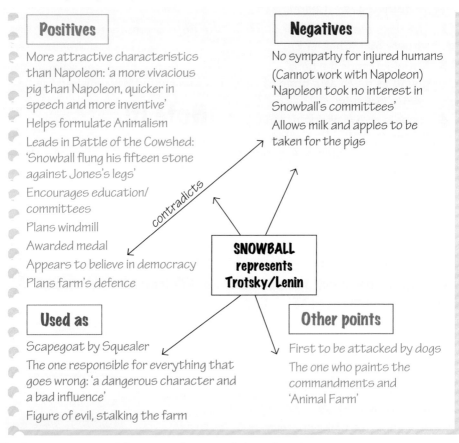

Positives

More attractive characteristics than Napoleon: 'a more vivacious pig than Napoleon, quicker in speech and more inventive'
Helps formulate Animalism
Leads in Battle of the Cowshed: 'Snowball flung his fifteen stone against Jones's legs'
Encourages education/ committees
Plans windmill
Awarded medal
Appears to believe in democracy
Plans farm's defence

Negatives

No sympathy for injured humans (Cannot work with Napoleon) 'Napoleon took no interest in Snowball's committees'
Allows milk and apples to be taken for the pigs

contradicts

SNOWBALL represents Trotsky/Lenin

Used as

Scapegoat by Squealer
The one responsible for everything that goes wrong: 'a dangerous character and a bad influence'
Figure of evil, stalking the farm

Other points

First to be attacked by dogs
The one who paints the commandments and 'Animal Farm'

2. Create your own ideas map for one of the other characters.

Quick quiz

Answer these quick questions about the characters.

1. At the end, what does Squealer have difficulty doing because he is so fat?
2. Who raises the alarm when Boxer is being taken away?
3. What are Boxer's two favourite sayings?
4. Which animal is obsessed with her looks?
5. Who represents religion?

6. Which animal is cynical?

7. Napoleon is described as 'a large, rather fierce-looking …' what?

8. What is Snowball's ruthless comment when it looks as if Boxer has killed the stable-lad?

9. Who trains the sheep to bleat 'Four legs good, two legs better'?

10. Which farmer tricks Napoleon over the sale of the timber?

11. Which farm animal, apart from Mollie and Moses, appears to do nothing to support the revolution?

12. Who is honoured with a medal after the Battle of the Windmill?

13. Complete this quotation, which sums up Old Major's philosophy: 'All men are … All animals are …'

14. What is the name of Napoleon's solicitor?

15. Who is 'a sly-looking man in a low-crowned bowler hat'?

16. Which animal protects the ducklings at the start of the novel?

17. How much of the alphabet does Clover manage to learn?

18. Who in history does Pilkington represent?

19. What song does Old Major teach the animals?

20. What does Napoleon have a reputation for always getting?

Power paragraphs

Write **a paragraph** in response to **each of these questions**. For each, try to **use one quotation** you have learned from this section.

1. What part does Mollie play in the story?

2. Why are the dogs essential to Napoleon's dictatorship?

Exam practice

Re-read the two paragraphs beginning on page 23 in Chapter 4 with 'Most of this time …' and ending on page 24 with '… Frederick and Pilkington said'.

What do these paragraphs tell you about Frederick and Pilkington? Write **two paragraphs** explaining your ideas.

You could comment on:

● how Frederick and Pilkington are described, and what they think and do in these paragraphs

● how Orwell presents Frederick and Pilkington in these paragraphs.

THEMES Power and corruption

Five key things about power and corruption

Animal Farm does not just mirror the Russian Revolution – it is about dictatorships in a more general sense, too.

1. **Lord Acton**, a nineteenth-century **British politician**, said 'All power tends to corrupt and absolute power corrupts absolutely.' This happens in the novel.
2. Both Jones and Napoleon use their power corruptly so the animals **suffer**.
3. Jones is **violent** and **uncaring**; Napoleon uses **terror**, **propaganda** and **lies** to maintain his position.
4. Napoleon **rewrites history** to boost his reputation and control the animals, ending up working with the enemy – the humans.
5. The **Soviet collective farms** should have provided a good standard of living – but instead, workers were **exploited**. It is the same on Animal Farm.

In what ways is Jones corrupt?

- Jones owns the farm but mistreats his animals (as do Frederick and Pilkington).
- He exploits animals for profit – their lives are miserable.
- He even fires his gun to stop the animals' noise.

What does Napoleon do to maintain his power?

- Napoleon's dogs suppress any dissent.
- He employs Squealer to convince the animals with lies.
- History is rewritten so he is presented as responsible for the victories (**'Comrade Napoleon sprang forward with a cry of "Death to Humanity!"'**) and the farm's development.

To what extent is Napoleon corrupt?

- He betrays the revolution, taking the gains and growing fat on the profits.
- He too exploits the animals, selling eggs, and selling Boxer to the knacker.
- He breaks the commandments.
- He ends up a friend to the humans, **symbolically** even looking like them and **'casting haughty glances from side to side'**.

Five key quotations

1. The farm is a frightening place under Jones: **'every one of you will scream your lives out at the block within a year'** (Chapter 1)

2. The pigs take the milk and apples: **'"Never mind the milk, comrades," cried Napoleon'** (Chapter 2)

3. Napoleon's bodyguards: **'enormous dogs wearing brass-studded collars'** with **'snapping jaws'** (Chapter 5)

4. Napoleon is elevated above the other animals: **'He was always referred to in formal style as "our Leader, Comrade Napoleon"'** (Chapter 8)

5. The pigs start to look and dress like humans: **'Napoleon himself appeared in a black coat, rat-catcher breeches, and leather leggings'** (Chapter 10)

Note it!

Notice how the intellectual power of the pigs allows them to become leaders – the way they learn to read and write, and their ability to plan and organise enables them to become leaders and tyrants.

Exam focus

How can I write about the corruption of the pigs? (AO1)

You can show how Snowball seems to care about the animals, while Napoleon turns into a self-interested tyrant.

Although he is not perfect, Snowball does think about the wellbeing of the animals. In contrast, Napoleon	Topic sentence introduces the point
cares only for himself. He uses the dogs to terrorise the animals: 'enormous dogs wearing brass-studded collars'. In addition, through Squealer he effectively	Point is further explained
rewrites history and establishes a personality cult around him, so that he is acclaimed and reaps all the	Appropriate supporting quotation
benefits as dictator at the farm.	Extends the point

Now you try!

Finish this paragraph about how the pigs are just as corrupt as the humans. Use one of the quotations from the list.

By the end of the novel, the pigs are as corrupt as Jones, Pilkington and Frederick, even dressing similarly, as ....

My progress Needs more work ☐ Getting there ☐ Sorted! ☐   43

THEMES Freedom and equality

Five key things about freedom and equality

When Jones has gone, the animals think they have freedom and equality, but the pigs replace him.

1. Orwell shows that putting Old Major's dream into practice is not easy.
2. The society seems relatively **equal** after the revolution, but that does not last.
3. The **hierarchy** among the animals is based on **intelligence**.
4. The novel shows that the **problem** is not humans but **greed**.
5. An equal society is set up in the novel as the **ideology** behind Animalism – but Orwell soon reveals that it will always be the case that **'some animals are more equal than others'**.

How does Old Major see equality?

- He thinks that with the humans gone, tyranny will end.
- He believes that the animals will share the fruits of their labours and work together as 'comrades'.
- He states that **'All animals are equal'**.

Why does Old Major's dream fail?

- Not all the animals are committed to the dream or even friendly to each other – for example, it is easy to train the dogs as executioners.
- There is a hierarchy on the farm, and the pigs' intelligence makes them leaders: they can then do what they like.

What happens to the animals' freedom?

- Initially, there is more food and they dream of an easier life.
- Napoleon increasingly terrorises the animals, and they suffer as his plans fail. They work longer hours for less food and are **'generally hungry'**.
- 'Beasts of England' and animal committees are banned and Old Major's skull, which represents Animalism, is buried.

Five key quotations

1. Old Major's dream: 'among us animals let there be perfect unity, perfect comradeship in the struggle' (Chapter 1)

2. He believes in equality: 'Weak or strong, clever or simple, we are all brothers.' (Chapter 1)

3. Their initial freedom brings joy: 'The animals were happy as they had never conceived it possible to be.' (Chapter 3)

4. Freedom and equality have totally gone when the pigs carry whips: 'it did not seem strange when ... the pigs ... all carried whips in their trotters' (Chapter 10)

5. The one remaining commandment says: 'All animals are equal but some animals are more equal than others' (Chapter 10)

Note it!

Notice how the animals' lives change for the better immediately after Jones's departure, and how they feel about their newfound freedom.

Exam focus

How can I write about the idea of equality in the novel? AO1

You can begin with Old Major's speech and explain how the animals are affected by their freedom at first.

Old Major's dream of equality, with all animals free, is the ideology on which Animal Farm is established. He believes all animals can be comrades: 'Weak or strong, clever or simple, we are all brothers.' His appeal is inclusive, offering freedom and hope to the many, and immediately after the take-over, it all seems perfect. The animals gambol around the fields with joy and, freed of Jones, they ensure there is no wastage in the harvest.

- Topic sentence introduces the point
- Point is further explained
- Appropriate supporting quotation
- Further development of point

Now you try!

Finish this paragraph about how unequal life is for the animals on Manor Farm at the end of the novel. Use one of the quotations from the list.

By the end of the novel, the one remaining commandment no longer states that all animals are equal ....

Five key things about oppression and violence

Napoleon's control is based on oppression of the animals, backed up by the threat of violence.

1. After the revolution, the animals have a sense of **equality**, but that ends as the pigs' **powers increase**.
2. When Napoleon unleashes the **dogs**, their **violence** terrifies the animals, thus ending any meaningful opposition.
3. The animals suffer **oppression** as their rights are removed.
4. The threat of violence is supported by **deceit** as the animals lose all their freedoms.
5. By the end, the animals' lives are **worse** than in the time of Jones.

In what ways are the animals oppressed?

- With Snowball gone, the Sunday morning meetings end so the animals no longer have a say in how the farm is run.
- No dissent is allowed: animals are executed in the barn to serve as a warning to others.
- The commandments are changed, so that the pigs can act however they like – for example, animals can be killed.
- The animals' labour in the fields **'was as it had always been'**. The hens rebel to save their eggs, but Napoleon acts **'swiftly and ruthlessly'**.
- The pigs get fatter, but the other animals have less to eat and no improved quality of life.

How much violence is there on Animal Farm?

- The extreme way the dogs drive Snowball off the farm terrifies the animals.
- The hens are starved into submission – Napoleon says any animal who gives them food **'should be punished by death'**.
- In the purge, four pigs, three hens, a goose and three sheep are slaughtered.
- Boxer is taken to the knacker's when he is no longer of use.
- The pigs carry whips, signalling their violent nature.

Five key quotations

1. When the meetings stop: 'the animals were dismayed by this announcement' (Chapter 5)
2. Four pigs are executed for opposing Napoleon: 'the dogs ... seized four of the pigs by the ear and dragged them, squealing with pain and terror, to Napoleon's feet' (Chapter 7)
3. After the executions: 'the air was heavy with the smell of blood' (Chapter 7)
4. The animals' lives are hard: 'They were generally hungry, they slept on straw, they drank from the pool, they laboured in the fields ...' (Chapter 10)
5. Pilkington's opinion: 'the lower animals on Animal Farm did more work and received less food than any animals in the country' (Chapter 10)

Note it!

Notice how the animals react to the executions. This is when the violence is at its worst, and although they continue to dream everything seems to have changed for them.

Exam focus

How can I write about oppression in *Animal Farm*?

You can examine all the pigs' actions which limit the animals' freedom, burden them and reduce the quality of their lives.

> After the revolution, the animals' lives improve – but that ends as they are increasingly exploited by the pigs and persuaded to work harder: 'They were generally hungry, they slept on straw, they drank from the pool, they laboured in the fields'. The freedoms they thought they had won are taken from them and Napoleon's reign of terror keeps them in line while the pigs live in style.

Topic sentence introduces the point

Appropriate supporting quotation

Further development of ideas

Now you try!

Finish this paragraph about how violence or the threat of violence is used to keep the animals in order. Use one of the quotations from the list.

When the executions take place, Orwell shows how the animals are cowed into submission by Napoleon's violence, which extends even to pigs ....

My progress   Needs more work ☐   Getting there ☐   Sorted! ☐

Five key things about education and learning

In *Animal Farm*, we see that those with most intelligence control others.

1. There is a saying that 'knowledge is power': the **pigs** use their **knowledge** to wield **power** on the farm.
2. Their **intellectual ability** is reflected in how they **learn** to read and write. They are able to design the windmill and enter into trade agreements.
3. They use their intellectual ability to **persuade** and **deceive** the animals, e.g. by adapting the commandments to their needs.
4. The other animals **struggle** with ideas, so cannot **argue** effectively.
5. Possibly only Benjamin has the **understanding** to see how the pigs are **manipulating** the animals.

How is Snowball involved in educating the animals?

- At first, with the other pigs, Snowball helps educate the other animals about what the revolution will mean.
- Snowball is the best writer, so he paints the simplified commandments.
- He sets up Animal Committees to share views, and reading and writing classes.

What do the pigs do with their learning?

- The pigs learn skills and **'other necessary arts'** from books.
- Snowball studies Caesar's campaigns to prepare for Jones's attack, *Electricity for Beginners* to help him plan the windmill, and *Farmer and Stockbreeder*.

- Becoming more human, the pigs order the *Daily Mirror* and magazines to read.

What are the other animals' limitations?

- Only Benjamin and Muriel can read effectively.
- Clover learns the whole alphabet; Boxer can only manage four letters.
- Most animals cannot get further than the letter A. These limitations are reflected in their inability to think clearly. The pigs use this weakness to control them.

Five key quotations

1. Snowball tries to educate the animals: 'He was indefatigable at this.' (Chapter 3)
2. The pigs learn rapidly: 'As for the pigs, they could already read and write perfectly.' (Chapter 3)
3. Most of the animals are intellectually limited: 'None of the other animals on the farm could get further than the letter A.' (Chapter 3)
4. Squealer convinces the animals easily because they cannot read: 'Have you any record of such a resolution? Is it written down anywhere?' (Chapter 6)
5. Persuading them that Snowball was a traitor, Squealer again uses the animals' illiteracy against them: 'I could show you this in his own writing, if you were able to read it' (Chapter 7)

Note it!

Note the attempts made by Snowball to educate the animals, but also his general lack of success with this.

Exam focus

How can I write about the pigs' use of their educational advantage? (AO1)

You can show how easily the pigs deceive the animals who cannot read, or who have poor memories or limited reasoning skills.

The animals are easily convinced by Squealer because they never seem to have an adequate response to anything he says. When he says, 'I could show you this in his own writing if you were able to read,' it seems unanswerable. Also, when the pigs change the commandments, slight but important alterations in wording are accepted by the animals, who think they must have misremembered what was there before.

Topic sentence introduces the point

Point is further explained using an embedded quotation

Extension using linked point

Now you try!

Finish this paragraph about how the pigs educate themselves so that they are in a perfect position to run the farm. Use one of the quotations from the list.

After Old Major explains his dream, the pigs begin to learn by using an old spelling book, and soon . . . .

THEMES Language and propaganda

Five key things about language and propaganda

In his essay *Politics and the English Language*, Orwell says, 'Political language is designed to make lies sound truthful and murder respectable'. For the pigs, language is power.

1. Squealer delivers **propaganda** on behalf of Napoleon.
2. He uses **persuasive rhetoric**, **false facts** and **dire warnings** as persuasion.
3. The animals regularly find his arguments **'unanswerable'**.
4. Adjustments in language allow the pigs to **change the commandments**, and even the meaning of 'equal' is changed: it is impossible to be **'more equal'**.
5. **'Comrade'** was intended to represent real equality: the word is **banned** by the end.

How does Squealer use language to persuade the animals?

- He uses rhetorical statements to convince the animals: **'Our Leader, Comrade Napoleon ... has stated categorically – categorically, comrade – that Snowball was Jones's agent'**. He also uses **rhetorical questions** to challenge the animals – for example, when the debates are ended.

- When explaining the pigs' work, he purposely chooses words the animals cannot understand, from the business world, such as **'files'** and **'memoranda'**.

When do the pigs rely on propaganda?

- The blame for negative events is laid at Snowball's feet, while Napoleon is presented as the hero so that he represents everything positive – even when his plans fail.

- Squealer justifies what is unfair: when the pigs take the milk, he explains they need it because it is good for them.

- When the animals feel their life is harder than ever, Squealer feeds them invented statistics.

- The commandments are changed to justify the pigs' evil; and the bleating of the sheep is used as a tool to cover up unrest or, at the end, to make the pigs' human characteristics acceptable (**'four legs better'**).

Five key quotations

1. Squealer can convince the animals of anything: **'he could turn black into white'** (Chapter 2)

2. He uses rhetorical questions: **'Surely, comrades, you do not want Jones back?'** (Chapter 5)

3. When times are hard, Squealer's linguistic skill is used to encourage the workers: **'Squealer made excellent speeches on the joy of service and the dignity of labour'** (Chapter 7)

4. The use of statistics: **'every class of foodstuff had increased by 200 per cent, 300 per cent, or 500 per cent'** (Chapter 8)

5. Language creates positive, elevated impressions of Napoleon: **'always referred to in formal style as "our Leader, Comrade Napoleon"'** (Chapter 8)

Note it!

Notice how many times Squealer convinces the animals that all is well and Napoleon's plans will prove successful, e.g. when the second windmill is destroyed, he claims it is a victory: 'Have we not driven the enemy off our soil?'

Exam focus

How can I write about the pigs' use of propaganda? AO2

You can write about Squealer's use of false facts, and how he 'reinvents' history and even the animals' reality.

It is said of Squealer that 'he could turn black into white', and this makes him the perfect mouthpiece for the pigs' propaganda. Napoleon uses him to change the animals' memories of Snowball, mould his own image as their hero and justify the animals' hardships, using fake statistics and persuasive language to make them think positively about their leader and the prospects of the farm.

Embedded quotation incorporated into topic sentence

Topic sentence introduces idea

Development, using examples

Now you try!

Finish this paragraph about how Squealer uses the threat of Jones's return to lead the animals to accept worsening conditions. Use one of the quotations from the list.

Squealer has a range of persuasive techniques, but his use of rhetorical questions, such as ....

THEMES Community

Community

Five key things about community

Most of the animals work well as a group, and function as a community.

1. The **pigs** and the **dogs** are clearly different from the rest, as they hold the **power** and have **privileges**.
2. Most of the other animals **care for each other**.
3. With the exception of Benjamin, all the animals expect an **improved** standard of life once Jones has gone.
4. The animals work **sixty hours** a week on the crops and **toil** together to build the windmills.
5. As a group, they have their hard-won **rights taken away** by the pigs.

How is the sense of community created by Orwell?

- The sense of community is first revealed when all the animals attend Old Major's meeting. At first they meet regularly, sing 'Beasts of England' together and are allowed to make decisions.
- With the exception of Mollie, the cat and Moses, they work together to make a better future for all.
- They all fight in the battles of the Cowshed and the Windmill.
- They all fall under the pigs' reign of terror, suffering hardships and disappointments together.

How does Orwell emphasise the animals' togetherness?

- Orwell regularly refers to them as **'the animals'**, identifying them as a group.
- At Old Major's meeting, they enter as a group. Clover **symbolically** protects the weak – the ducklings.
- There is a communal sense of shock when the dogs execute those opposed to Napoleon.
- When Boxer is taken away, all the animals try to save him.

- At the end, excluded from the farmhouse, they all peer through the window as Napoleon welcomes the humans. They represent the oppressed majority, or outsiders.

Five key quotations

1. Old Major's rallying cry: **'Weak or strong, clever or simple, we are all brothers.'** (Chapter 1)

2. After the revolution: **'remembering the glorious things that had happened, they all raced out into the pasture together'** (Chapter 2)

3. Delighted with their farm: **'food was an acute positive pleasure, now that it was truly their own food'** (Chapter 3)

4. After the executions: **'The animals huddled about Clover, not speaking.'** (Chapter 7)

5. The animals' togetherness is emphasised again when Napoleon emerges with a whip: **'amazed, terrified, huddling together'** (Chapter 10)

Note it!

Identify what Old Major has to say about equality when he describes how the animals must work together to displace the humans and create a brighter future. Note the phrases he uses.

Exam focus

How can I write about how the idea of community is presented?

You can write about how the animals care for each other, work and suffer together.

> Orwell represents the animals as oppressed by Jones, but shows their spirit as they rise together to drive him away to create a more egalitarian community. They are all equals: Weak or strong, clever or simple, we are all brothers.' They are prepared to work long hours together to make Animal Farm a success, in the belief that they will have a richer future with good food and time for leisure.

Topic sentence introduces the point

Supporting quotation embedded

Development of idea

Now you try!

Finish this paragraph about how Napoleon betrays Old Major's ideas of community. Use one of the quotations from the list.

In contrast to the earlier ideals of equality in their community, Orwell shows the animals' shocked reaction when Napoleon ....

My progress   Needs more work ☐   Getting there ☐   Sorted! ☐

1. Look at this idea map about the pigs' corruption. Is there anything else you could add?

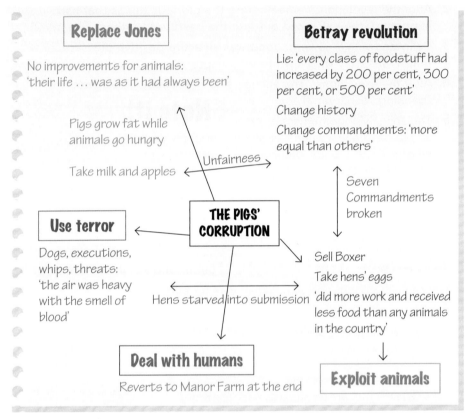

Replace Jones

No improvements for animals: 'their life ... was as it had always been'

Pigs grow fat while animals go hungry

Take milk and apples

Betray revolution

Lie: 'every class of foodstuff had increased by 200 per cent, 300 per cent, or 500 per cent'

Change history

Change commandments: 'more equal than others'

Unfairness

Seven Commandments broken

THE PIGS' CORRUPTION

Use terror

Dogs, executions, whips, threats: 'the air was heavy with the smell of blood'

Hens starved into submission

Sell Boxer

Take hens' eggs

'did more work and received less food than any animals in the country'

Deal with humans

Reverts to Manor Farm at the end

Exploit animals

2. Create your own ideas map about another of the novel's theme.

Quick quiz

Answer these quick questions about the themes.

1. How is Napoleon referred to?
2. Where are the animals when Napoleon is making his speech to the humans?
3. What is it about the dogs' collars that make them seem threatening?
4. How many letters can Boxer remember?
5. Apart from the pigs, which two animals can read best?

6. Who tries to educate the animals?
7. How does Snowball learn about electricity?
8. Squealer purposely uses some words the animals cannot understand. Name two.
9. How does Jones disrupt Old Major's meeting?
10. To support the changes in the pigs at the end, what are the sheep trained to do?
11. Which three animals do not help the others in their work after the revolution?
12. Quote a statistic that Squealer uses to convince the animals.
13. Pigs, hens and sheep are executed in the barn. Which other animal is killed at the same time?
14. After the executions, what smell is in the air?
15. What song is banned by the pigs?
16. Old Major's skull is a symbol of the Animalist ideals. What happens to it at the end?
17. What physical changes do the pigs undergo that signals their corruption?
18. When things go wrong, how does Napoleon avoid responsibility?
19. What does Pilkington say impresses him about Animal Farm?
20. Which animal seems to know that the pigs are manipulating them?

Power paragraphs

Write **a paragraph** in response to **each of these questions**. For each, try to **use one quotation** you have learned from this section.

1. In what ways is Jones's behaviour harmful to his animals?
2. How is life better for the animals immediately after the revolution?

Exam practice

Re-read what Napoleon says to his guests on page 89 in Chapter 10 from 'He too, he said …' to … 'the prosperity of the Manor Farm!'

To what extent has corruption triumphed at Animal Farm? Write **two paragraphs** explaining your ideas.

You could comment on:

● the ways in which life has reverted to how it used to be
● how Napoleon's attitude towards the animals and the humans is shown.

LANGUAGE Imagery and vocabulary

Five key things about imagery and vocabulary

1. Orwell's novel was originally subtitled 'A Fairy Tale' – he uses **simple language** to put across **key messages**.
2. Its **short sentences** reflect the language in children's stories.
3. This simple language is appropriate for a story in which most characters are **anthropomorphic**, i.e. the farm animals' **linguistic ability** is **limited**.
4. The novel uses **imagery** and relies heavily on **symbolism**.
5. Orwell understands the **power of language** and how it can **manipulate** thoughts and beliefs. In this case it is how the pigs control the other animals.

In what ways is the language simple?

- From the opening, simple vocabulary is used: **'Mr Jones, of the Manor Farm, had locked the hen-houses for the night ...'**.
- Actions and reactions of the animals are presented simply: **'Clover and Benjamin warned him to take care of his health ...'**.
- Boxer's two mottoes, one being **'I will work harder'**, indicate the simplicity of the animals' thoughts.

How is imagery used effectively?

- Animals' characteristics are captured in a short sentence, e.g. **'Clover was a stout motherly mare'**.
- The farm is described using **evocative** vocabulary, e.g. **'they cropped mouthfuls of the sweet summer grass'**; the pigs' actions are a contrast (**'the air was heavy with the smell of blood'**).
- To reinforce his point, Orwell uses one **simile** repeatedly: the animals are **'like slaves'**.

How do the pigs use language powerfully?

- Squealer uses **rhetoric**, statistics and **vocabulary** the animals do not understand.
- They use the word **'comrade'**, suggesting all are part of a cooperative effort.

Five key quotations

1. The simplicity of the animals' thoughts – Boxer's motto: **'Napoleon is always right'** (Chapter 6)
2. Short, precise descriptions: **'Napoleon was a large, rather fierce-looking Berkshire boar'** (Chapter 2)
3. Recurring simile: **'The animals worked like slaves'** (Chapter 6)
4. Squealer's persuasive rhetoric: **'Surely, comrades, you do not want Jones back?'** (Chapter 5)
5. Contrast between the lives of the pigs and the other animals – at the end, while the animals are **'stricken'**, the pigs celebrate: **'There was the same hearty cheering as before'** (Chapter 10)

Note it!

Note the rich and sensory vocabulary used to describe the farm in Chapter 2 (e.g. **'They ... snuffed its rich scent'**) as Orwell shows the beauty of the animals' environment.

Exam focus

How can I write about vocabulary choices in the novel? AO2

You can write about Orwell's presentation of characters and events: how he uses the words the characters speak.

Orwell keeps the vocabulary simple in Animal Farm because he is telling an uncomplicated story while putting across important messages. When Boxer says, 'Napoleon is always right', the simple way he expresses his ideas demonstrates his limited intelligence. The reader is aware of the lack of flexibility in Boxer's thinking, but it also makes the narrative easily accessible to all.

Topic sentence introduces the point

Appropriate supporting quotation

Explanation of technique

Development of language point

Now you try!

Finish this paragraph about how the harshness of life on the farm is described. Use one of the quotations from the list.

To reveal how the animals are oppressed, Orwell uses a recurring simile . . . .

LANGUAGE Narrative style

Five key things about narrative style

1. The **narrative** style is the way the narrator or author addresses the reader.
2. Animal Farm begins with an **omniscient**, all-seeing **narrator**.
3. Most of the story is told in a **detached way** but from the **perspective** of the animals. On two occasions we are given Clover's thoughts.
4. While the story opens like a **traditional children's story**, many of its events are **harrowing**.
5. In seeing the animals' **confusion** and **distress**, we **empathise** with them.

What is Orwell's narrative style?

- Generally Orwell uses short sentences, as in a children's story, though his message about the abuse of power is aimed at adults and is more powerful because of the way the story is told.

- Initially, we learn exactly what is happening, even behind the farmhouse's closed doors as Jones **'drew himself a last glass of beer from the barrel in the scullery'**.

- Later, everything is described from the animals' viewpoint – the reader is left to deduce what exactly the pigs have been doing.

- The reader's sympathy is engaged when Orwell describes Clover's thoughts in detail.

How are the events described?

- The narrative is **chronological** with events unfolding in time order.
- At first, the events are described in detail; by the time the pigs have total control of the farm, things move on much more rapidly: e.g. **'The seasons came and went, the short animal lives fled by.'** This is because Orwell largely focuses on how the pigs attain their power.
- When the novel opens, Jones is in his house and the animals congregate in the barn. Significantly, at the end, the animals are outside looking in as Napoleon entertains his neighbours. The plot has come full circle.

Five key quotations

1. Simple narrative style: 'It had been agreed they should all meet in the big barn' (Chapter 1)
2. Omniscient narrator: 'he ... made his way up to bed, where Mrs. Jones was already snoring' (Chapter 1)
3. The reader's sympathies are with the animals: 'Boxer's face, with the white stripe down his nose, appeared at the small window at the back of the van' (Chapter 9)
4. Clover's thoughts are revealed: 'It was not for this that they had built the windmill and faced the bullets of Jones's guns.' (Chapter 7)
5. The reader sees through the animals' eyes: 'They tiptoed up to the house, and ... peered in at the dining-room window' (Chapter 10)

Note it!

Notice how Orwell creates sympathy for Clover and the animals immediately after the executions. Identify Clover's different thoughts and decide how Orwell expects the reader to react.

Exam focus

How can I write about Orwell's narrative style?

You can write about how the way the story is told affects the reader's response.

The events described seem even more horrific since, due to Orwell's simple style, they are unexpected. He reveals how the animals' dreams are destroyed: 'It was not for this they had built the windmill and faced the bullets of Jones's guns.' To generate sympathy for the animals, Orwell uses a detached narrative style but focuses on the animals' viewpoint. This allows the reader to see things from their perspective and make judgements on the action.

Topic sentence introduces the point

Appropriate supporting quotation

Explanation of narrative technique

Now you try!

Finish this paragraph about how Orwell generates sympathy for the animals at the end. Use one of the quotations from the list.

Orwell shows that the animals are as excluded at the end as they were at the start, placing them outside the celebration ....

LANGUAGE Mood and atmosphere

Three key things about mood

1. The tale first offers **hope**, but evokes a **mood** of **disillusionment** at the end when Benjamin's pessimism is proved correct.
2. Old Major sets out a **positive vision**, and when Jones is driven out the animals celebrate.
3. The hope and joy pass as the pigs tighten their **control**; **ironically**, the atmosphere is increasingly grim and life actually becomes **harder**.

What is the mood when Jones has gone?

- The language is poetic, appealing to the senses, as the animals delight in **'sweet summer grass'**.
- The animals are happy, taking pride in their work and its rewards: **'Every mouthful of food was an acute positive pleasure'**.
- This mood soon changes: e.g. there is dismay over the executions and panic when Boxer is taken away.

How does Orwell use irony?

- The **irony** is that the warnings that Old Major gives about Jones's behaviour can increasingly be applied to the pigs.
- **'Spontaneous demonstrations'** are actually organised by the pigs.
- There are songs and speeches on the farm, but they are intended to distract the animals from the reality of day-to-day hardships.
- The animals may be proud they are not working for **'idle, thieving human beings'** but the reader is aware that they are actually working only for the benefit of their new masters – the pigs.

What is the mood at the end?

- The mood is one of **tragedy**.
- After the executions, the loss of Boxer and the transformation of the pigs into humans, the reader is expected to understand the irony of what has happened.
- The animals' exclusion in the final scene **symbolises** the revolution's failure.

Three key quotations

1. Delight after evicting Jones: 'they gambolled round and round, they hurled themselves into the air in great leaps of excitement' (Chapter 2)

2. Dismay as Boxer is taken away: '**A cry of horror burst from all the animals.**' (Chapter 9)

3. Verbs indicating the animals' mood at the end: '**Amazed, terrified, huddling together**' (Chapter 10)

Quick quiz

1. The story is told simply. What was its original subtitle?
2. Why do the pigs use the term 'comrade'?
3. What sort of narration does Orwell use at the beginning?
4. Which animal's thoughts are narrated after the executions?
5. Events are presented in the order they happen over time. What do we call that sort of order?
6. Quote three words to describe how the animals feel after the executions.
7. What is evocative vocabulary?
8. Overall, why is Old Major's speech ironic?
9. What is ironic about 'spontaneous demonstrations' on the farm?
10. How would you describe the animals' mood just after the revolution and at the end of the novel?

Power paragraphs

Write **two paragraphs** explaining how Squealer's use of language convinces the animals through a) rhetoric and b) complicated vocabulary.

EXAM PRACTICE Understanding the exam

Five key things about the exam

1. You need to answer **one** question from a **choice of two** on *Animal Farm*.

2. It will focus on **Orwell's exploration** of an aspect of the novel, such as a **character**, **relationship** or **theme**, and how he **presents** it.

3. You will have about **45–50 minutes** to read and respond to the question.

4. There are **30 marks** for the question, which assesses **AOs 1, 2 and 3**. Remember that **AO3** relates to '**context**'.

5. You can also gain a further **4 marks** for **AO4**: your use of **spelling, punctuation and grammar**.

What will a question look like?

You must explain Orwell's techniques

1. What methods does Orwell use to present Napoleon as an evil character?

   Write about:
   - what Napoleon does that is evil
   - the methods Orwell uses to reveal Napoleon's evil.

   [30 marks]
   AO4 [4 marks]

This is the focus of your answer

You must refer to specific actions or events

A reminder to watch your use of spelling, punctuation, vocabulary and grammar

Do all questions look the same?

- Not all questions will begin this way. Some might contain statements you must argue with or against. For example, **'Not all the pigs are the same. Snowball actually cares about the other animals.'** How far do you agree with this statement?

- Some questions might ask you about a **relationship** between two characters, for example between Napoleon and Snowball.

What do I need to do to get a good mark?

Use this grid to understand what your current level is and how to improve it:

	AO1 Read, understand, respond	AO2 Analyse language, form, structure and effects	AO3 Show understanding of contexts
High	• You make **precise references** to the focuses of the question. • Your argument is **well-structured**, with quotations **fluently embedded** in sentences.	• You **analyse** and **interpret** the methods Orwell uses **very effectively**. • You **explore thoughtfully** the effects of these on the reader. • You show **excellent use** of subject terminology.	• You make **detailed, relevant links** between specific elements of the novel and social, historical contexts.
Mid	• You make a **range of references** to the focuses of the question. • You respond in **a clear, logical way** with **relevant** quotations chosen.	• You **explain clearly** some of the methods Orwell uses, and **some effects** on the reader. • You use **mostly relevant** subject terminology.	• You show **clear evidence** of understanding context, which is **linked** to the novel in places.
Lower	• You make **some references** to the focus of the question, but in rather a patchy way. • You make **some useful points** but evidence is **not always clear or relevant**.	• You make **occasional attempts** to explain Orwell's methods, but these are a little **unclear**. • You show **some use** of subject terminology.	• You demonstrate **basic awareness** of context, but **links** to the novel are **undeveloped** and **not always relevant**.

AO4 For top marks: use a **range** of vocabulary and sentence structures, adopt a **clear, purposeful and effective** writing style, and make sure your spelling and punctuation is **accurate**.

Read these exam-style character questions

Here are three further examples of **single character** questions, plus one about character '**types**'.

2. 'Boxer ... never lost heart.' What is Boxer's value to the farm?

   Write about:
   - what Boxer does that is of value
   - how Orwell shows Boxer's value.

   [30 marks]
   AO4 [4 marks]

3. How far do you agree with the view that Snowball is treated in a way he does not deserve?

   Write about:
   - what Snowball does and what happens to him
   - how Orwell presents Snowball as a character who is unfairly treated.

   [30 marks]
   AO4 [4 marks]

4. 'Squealer is an essential ally who helps Napoleon gain control of the farm.' How far do you agree with this statement?

   Write about:
   - what Squealer says and does
   - how Orwell presents Squealer as an ally helping Napoleon.

   [30 marks]
   AO4 [4 marks]

5. How far does Orwell present the humans in the novel as corrupt?

   Write about:
   - what the humans in the novel say and do
   - how far Orwell presents them as corrupt.

   [30 marks]
   AO4 [4 marks]

NOW read these further exam-style character questions

These three further questions are examples of another type of character question you might face. They deal with **relationships** between characters, or how the author presents characters in **different ways** from others.

6. How does Orwell highlight the differences between Napoleon and Snowball?

Write about:

- what is different between the two characters
- how the author presents these differences.

[30 marks]
AO4 [4 marks]

7. 'Benjamin is devoted to Boxer.'

How far is Benjamin presented as a good friend to Boxer?

Write about:

- what we learn of their friendship
- how Orwell presents the friendship.

[30 marks]
AO4 [4 marks]

8. 'The humans are too clever for Napoleon.'

How do Napoleon's relationships with the humans change and develop?

Write about:

- how Napoleon interacts with the humans
- how Orwell presents these relationships.

[30 marks]
AO4 [4 marks]

Five key stages to follow

1. **Read** the **question**; **highlight** key words.
2. Quickly **generate ideas** for your response.
3. **Plan** for paragraphs.
4. **Write** your response and **check it** against your plan as you progress.
5. **Check** for **AO4** as you progress (spelling, punctuation, vocabulary, etc.).

What do I focus on?

Highlight the **key words**:

> 2. 'Boxer … never lost heart.'
> What is Boxer's value to the farm?
> Write about:
> - what Boxer does that is of value
> - how Orwell shows Boxer's value.

What do they tell you? Focus on the novel as a whole, stick to what Boxer does to protect and improve Animal Farm, and explain Orwell's methods for presenting Boxer's contributions.

How do I get my ideas?

Note your ideas in an ideas map or list them in a table.

What Boxer does

Fights in the battles

'Animal Hero, First Class'

Does the heaviest work needed to build the windmills: 'the other animals found more inspiration in Boxer's strength'

Boxer's value

How Orwell shows his value

What the other animals think of him: 'Boxer was the admiration of everybody.'

Descriptions of Boxer: Remains loyal to the farm to the end: 'Boxer … never lost heart'

What Boxer does	How Orwell presents his value
• The hardest worker – longest hours • Does the heaviest work needed to build the windmills	• Medal for valour • Represents the working class: unending commitment • Remains loyal to the farm to the end

HOW do I structure my ideas?

Make a **plan** for **paragraphs**.* Decide the order for your points.

- Paragraph 1: Go straight into your first point: *Boxer's steadfast qualities are set out by Orwell at Old Major's meeting.*
- Paragraph 2: *How Boxer reacts immediately after the revolution (with Clover, the 'most faithful disciple').*
- Paragraph 3: *How he fights for the farm in the battles.*
- Paragraph 4: *His dedication to building the windmills, his general attitude ('I will work harder') and his trust in Napoleon.*
- Paragraph 5: *His ending and the emotions it prompts: 'Boxer was never seen again.'*

HOW do I write effectively?

Write clear, analytical points and try to embed your evidence fluently, e.g.

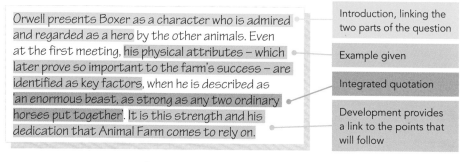

Orwell presents Boxer as a character who is admired and regarded as a hero by the other animals. Even at the first meeting, his physical attributes – which later prove so important to the farm's success – are identified as key factors, when he is described as 'an enormous beast, as strong as any two ordinary horses put together'. It is this strength and his dedication that Animal Farm comes to rely on.

Introduction, linking the two parts of the question

Example given

Integrated quotation

Development provides a link to the points that will follow

Now you try!

Re-read Question 3 on page 64 and plan your response in the same way.

*The plan above and the sample answers on pages 68 and 70 have five paragraphs, but you don't need to be limited to this if you have more points to include (and time to write them)!

What does a Grade 5 answer look like?

Read the task again, then the sample answer below.

2. 'Boxer … never lost heart.'

What is Boxer's value to the farm?

Write about:

- what Boxer does that is of value
- how Orwell shows Boxer's value.

[30 marks]

Boxer never gives up and so he is of great value to the farm. If he had not been there the farm might not have been a success. Right at the start when Old Major has his meeting, Orwell shows how strong he is when he says he can work really hard and this indicates to the reader he will be important. He actually says Boxer has 'tremendous powers' to stress how strong he is. This means that when the farm needs improving after Jones has gone Boxer will be the one to lead the work.

> **AO1** Clear opening, setting out of viewpoint
>
> **AO2** Identifies the writer's method with effective reference but no clear explanation
>
> **AO1** Reference with comment

After Jones's departure, Orwell describes Boxer and Clover as the 'most faithful disciples' of the revolution. This shows how the workhorses are vital to the pigs' and the farm's future, because the ones who are organising everything need the working class to do all the graft. For example, at harvest time they work the hardest. We are told that Boxer works from morning until night and gets up before everybody else so he can make an earlier start. He cannot learn more than four letters of the alphabet, but that does not matter as long as he continues to work physically.

> **AO1** Some understanding of effect on reader
>
> **AO3** Some understanding of context
>
> **AO1** Supports the explanation

Boxer fights for the farm too in a fearless way. He is awarded 'Animal Hero, First Class' after the Battle of the Windmill and leads the fight at the Battle of the Cowshed. This helps save Animal Farm. He knocks out the stable boy, even though it upsets him to do it. This makes the other men flee. He also hits several men on the head when Frederick attacks in the Battle of the Windmill. Orwell tells us this to show Boxer as a selfless hero.

> **AO1** Continuing clear response to task
>
> **AO4** Connectives would improve expression here
>
> **AO2** Understanding of writer's method

Boxer makes all this effort and promises 'I will work harder' because he is loyal to Napoleon and the revolution. After building the windmill the first time, he then does it again. The windmill represents the farm's future, and Boxer is the one who makes it possible. He even continues to work when he has a bad hoof. This represents the loyalty that the workers have to a revolutionary leader. Boxer never criticises Napoleon even if anything goes wrong.

— Paragraph 4

Boxer wears himself out to make the farm a success. He thinks he will live out a happy retirement but is betrayed when his usefulness ends. When he is taken away, the animals all panic because he is such an important figure to them. The image of Boxer in the van makes us feel great sympathy for him: 'the white stripe down his nose appeared at the small window at the back of the van'. After all that he has done, he has a tragic end. It is also ironic after what Old Major told him would happen if Jones stayed in charge: 'Boxer, the very day that those great muscles of yours lose their power, Jones will send you to the knacker'. And it happens under the pigs' rule – they do not value what he has done for them.

— Paragraph 5

Check the skills

Re-read paragraphs four and five of this response and:

- highlight the main **points** made
- circle any reference to **context**
- underline any **interpretations** the student has made.

Now you try!

Look again at paragraph three ('*Boxer fights bravely …*', etc.) and improve it by:

- Adding a **quotation** about how Boxer reacts to the injury to the stable-lad.
- **Explaining** what makes Boxer so fearless in the Battle of the Cowshed.
- Ending with a **summary point** about the strength and goodness of Boxer and how these have been **key ideas** through the novel.
- Improving the overall **style** by making sure your sentences **flow**; using **connectives** to **link** ideas.

What does a Grade 7+ answer look like?

Read the task again, then the sample answer below.

2. 'Boxer … never lost heart.' What is Boxer's value to the farm?

Write about:

● what Boxer does that is of value

● how Orwell shows Boxer's value.

[30 marks]

Just as the ordinary workers were central to the success of the Soviet Union, so Boxer's commitment to the revolution is essential to Animal Farm's survival and development. He is not the cleverest animal – only being able to learn four letters of the alphabet – but he never loses heart and effectively works himself to death so that the farm prospers. At Old Major's meeting, he is described as 'enormous' and as having 'tremendous powers of work': it is these qualities that Orwell highlights and which Boxer commits to the cause.

In his case, it is total commitment. Along with Clover, he is one of the most 'faithful disciples', implying that the revolution to him is like a religion, and from the first his attitude is reflected in his mantra: 'I will work harder'. Orwell allows him this succinct phrase because it is simple, which suits Boxer's character. He does not have a great intellect but has the outstanding work ethic and loyalty that Napoleon needs to bring his plans to fruition. Indeed, Boxer gets up 30 minutes before the others and labours unstintingly from morning until night.

It is not just his work that is essential, though. When the farm is under threat, he is arguably its main defender. After the Battle of the Cowshed, he is awarded 'Animal Hero, First Class' for his efforts; and during the Battle of the Windmill he strikes several men on the head, which is a significant factor in the animals' victory. Despite this, Orwell reveals what might ironically be called Boxer's humanity: he does not want to hurt anyone. His decency and compassion would be valued highly in any decent society; sadly, the pigs' tyranical regime does not see it as an asset.

AO3 Convincing comment to open

AO1 Thoughtful awareness of task

AO2 Includes writer's methods

AO3 Further analyses writer's method

AO1 Thoughtful analysis of ideas

AO1 Well-referenced throughout

AO4 Stong linking of ideas between paragraphs

AO2 Insightful comment on writer's method

AO1 Boxer's value successfully conceptualised

Of course, as years pass Boxer continues to work just as hard, ignoring the pain of his split hoof as he hauls stone from the quarry. Also, and crucially, whatever goes wrong he maintains his mantra that 'Napoleon is always right', which, in its blind obedience, is of enormous value to the pigs. Boxer is a kind of propaganda tool for them: like model labourers on the collective farms in the Soviet Union, he works as the pigs doubtless want every animal to work and they quote his maxim after his death.

Paragraph 4

Finally, Orwell engages the reader's sympathies for Boxer as he is taken away. The tragic image of his face 'with the white stripe down his nose … at the small window at the back of the van' is emotive and distressing. This is also heavily ironic, because in age he is valued no more by Napoleon than he would have been by Jones. Old Major warns him at the start: 'Boxer, the very day that those great muscles of yours lose their power, Jones will send you to the knacker': he never loses heart, but in the end he does lose his life – for nothing more than a case of whisky.

Paragraph 5

Check the skills

Re-read paragraphs four and five of this response and:

- identify any particularly **fluent** or **well-expressed ideas**
- highlight any places where the student has shown **deeper insight** and offered **original or particularly thoughtful ideas** or made **interesting links**
- find any further **references to context**.

Now you try!

Now, using the plan you wrote for Question 3 on page 67, write a full response. Here is a reminder of the question:

3. How far do you agree with the view that Snowball is treated in a way he does not deserve?

   Write about:

   - what Snowball does and what happens to him
   - how Orwell presents Snowball as a character who is unfairly treated.

   [30 marks]
   AO4 [4 marks]

9. It has been said that 'All power corrupts.'

   How far is this true in *Animal Farm*?

   Write about:

   - examples of corruption in the novel
   - how Orwell presents these examples.

   [30 marks]
   AO4 [4 marks]

10. What ideas about education does Orwell explore in the novel?

    Write about:

    - some ideas about education in the novel
    - how Orwell presents these ideas to the reader.

    [30 marks]
    AO4 [4 marks]

11. 'Orwell hated oppression.'

    How far does Orwell's presentation of the pigs support this view?

    Write about:

    - what the pigs say and do to oppress the other animals
    - how Orwell makes the reader feel about the oppression.

    [30 marks]
    AO4 [4 marks]

12. To what extent do we get a positive view of the animal community on Animal Farm?

    Write about:

    - how the animal community behaves
    - how Orwell presents positive and negative impressions of the animal community.

    [30 marks]
    AO4 [4 marks]

Now read these further theme questions

13. 'Some animals are more equal than others.'
How does *Animal Farm* show the truth in this statement?
Write about:
- what the novel has to say about some animals being more equal than others
- how Orwell presents equality and inequality.

[30 marks]
AO4 [4 marks]

14. 'All revolutions are doomed to fail.'
To what extent does Orwell explore this idea in the novel?
Write about:
- what happens after the revolution
- how Orwell presents some significant events after the revolution.

[30 marks]
AO4 [4 marks]

15. How do the pigs use language as a propaganda tool?
Write about:
- the messages they wish to put across
- how their choice of language persuades the other animals.

[30 marks]
AO4 [4 marks]

Five key stages to follow

1. **Read** the **question**; **highlight** key words.
2. Quickly **generate ideas** for your response.
3. **Plan** for paragraphs.
4. **Write** your response and **check** it against your plan as you progress.
5. **Check** for **AO4** as you progress (spelling, punctuation, vocabulary, etc.).

What do I focus on?

Highlight the **key words**:

9. It has been said that 'All power corrupts.'
   How far is this true in *Animal Farm*?
   Write about:
   ● examples of corruption in the novel
   ● how Orwell presents these examples.

What do they tell you? Focus on the novel as a whole, write about specific examples, explain what specific methods Orwell uses, and stick to the theme of how power corrupts and the reader's response to this.

How do I get my ideas?

Note your ideas in an ideas map or list them in a table.

Examples of corruption	How corruption is presented
Pigs become more like humans	Animals not able to recognise what's happening
Commandments changed: 'sleep in a bed … *with sheets*'	'It must be due to some fault in ourselves'
Squealer's lies 'could turn black into white'	Pigs gain all the benefits: Squealer – 'he could with difficulty see out of his eyes'

Corruption

Examples of corruption	How the corruption is presented
• Pigs become just like the humans, e.g. 'sleep in a bed with sheets' • Commandments change • Squealer's lies to cover up corruption: he 'could turn black into white'	• Other animals not able to recognise what is happening • Pigs gain all the benefits: 'Squealer was so fat that he could with difficulty see out of his eyes'

HOW do I structure my ideas?

Make a **plan** for **paragraphs**.* Decide the order for your points.

- Paragraph 1: *Draw links between Jones and the pigs and explain how Orwell provokes a reaction of empathy towards the oppressed animals.*
- Paragraph 2: *Corruption of the revolution/changes in commandments: 'sleep in a bed with sheets'.*
- Paragraph 3: *Oppression of the animals and violence towards them.*
- Paragraph 4: *Differences between Boxer and Napoleon – illustrate the corruption and its effects on the innocent.*
- Paragraph 5: *Final scenes as the pigs become human.*

HOW do I write effectively?

Write clear, analytical points and try to embed your evidence fluently, e.g.

The pigs' cruel treatment of the other animals leads the reader to empathise with their suffering. When the dogs carry out the executions in the barn, 'the air was heavy with the smell of blood', reminding the reader of the terrible violence on the farm under Jones. The word 'heavy' in particular contributes to the mood of oppression. Orwell implies the animals have escaped one life of horror only to be trapped in the corruption of another.

- Corruption and reaction of reader presented
- Integrated relevant quotation
- How the corruption is presented
- Summative content linking both bullets in the question

Now you try!

Re-read Question 10 on page 72 and plan your response in the same way.

*The plan above and the sample answers on pages 76 and 78 have five paragraphs, but you don't need to be limited to this if you have more points to include (and time to write them)!

What does a Grade 5 answer look like?

Read the task again, then the sample answer below.

9. It has been said that 'All power corrupts.'
   How is corruption shown in *Animal Farm*?
   Write about:
   - examples of corruption in the novel
   - how Orwell presents these examples.

   [30 marks]

Orwell's story proves that it does not matter who runs Animal Farm – because the pigs are as corrupt as Jones. Old Major tells the animals what's wrong with Jones's management, and the pigs go on to do the same things. This happened in Russia under the Tsar and then Stalin. Orwell expects us to feel sorry for the animals just as we should feel sympathy for the Russians suffering corruption. So when Major warns Boxer that Jones will send him to the knacker as soon as he loses his strength, it is ironic as that is exactly what the pigs do and they are his 'comrades'.

AO1 Clear opening statement

AO3 Awareness of context

AO2 Identifies method

As part of the corruption, the pigs change commandments to make their lives more comfortable. For example 'No animal shall sleep in a bed' becomes 'No animal shall sleep in a bed with sheets'. We are shocked at this, but sometimes Orwell expects us to laugh bitterly, such as when Squealer falls off the ladder altering a commandment and the animals still do not grasp what the pigs are doing. In fact, nobody except Benjamin knows what's actually happening. He's wise and knows the world has always been corrupt and a revolution won't improve it.

AO1 Good choice and use of close reference to novel

AO3 Clear understanding of ideas

The most corrupt thing the pigs do is kill their animal comrades. At the executions, 'the dogs ... seized four of the pigs by the ear and dragged them, squealing with pain'. The violence of the verbs here is upsetting. Another sign of corruption is how the animals are starved, while the pigs eat well. 'Never mind the milk, comrades' is what Napoleon shouts – but the pigs still get to drink it. In the end, the animals are as badly treated as they were under Jones. We pity them as they stand outside watching Napoleon's feast.

AO1 Sustains response to task

AO4 Choice of punctuation stresses the following point

AO1 Clarity on ideas, well supported

We can see how corrupt Napoleon is by comparing him with Boxer's honesty. Boxer is devoted to him, saying 'Napoleon is always right', and works all hours to make the farm a success. Orwell shows us how different and corrupt Napoleon is when he first drives out Snowball, like when Stalin forced Trotsky from Russia, and then uses his plans for the windmill as if the idea was his. By the end, Napoleon 'carried a whip in his trotter'. This all makes us weigh the honesty of Boxer against the corruption of Napoleon – who even sells Boxer so he can have a party and get drunk.

Paragraph 4

The tragedy of what happens on the farm is clearest at the end, when the pigs become friends with the humans and look more and more like them. Pilkington says that the animals 'did more work and received less food than any animals in the country'. This comparison ('more … less …') is intended to shock the reader, further making us realise that the pigs are now totally corrupt and the animals are worse off than those on other farms. We mostly sympathise with the animals like Clover, who is frightened even to get close to the house. The farm is back where it began and the revolution has failed.

Paragraph 5

Check the skills

Re-read paragraphs four and five of this response and:

- think of **two points of comparison** that could have been used in paragraph four to highlight Napoleon's corruption
- underline any **interpretations** the student has made
- find any **contextual** references.

Now you try!

Look again at paragraph three ('*The most corrupt thing the pigs do …*', etc.) and improve it by:

- Adding a **reference or quotation** about the harshness of the animals' lives.
- **Explaining** why the pigs execute the animals.
- Ending with a **summary point** expanding on our feelings for the animals and how this has been a **key idea** through the novel.
- Improving the overall **style** by making sure your sentences **flow**; using **connectives** to **link** ideas.

What does a Grade 7+ answer look like?

Read the task again, then the sample answer below.

9. It has been said that 'All power corrupts.'
   How is corruption shown in *Animal Farm*?
   Write about:
   - examples of corruption in the novel
   - how Orwell presents corruption to influence the reader's reactions to it.

   [30 marks]

Mr Jones, being a human, exploits the animals. The tragedy of Animal Farm is that the pigs behave in the same way and somehow seem more corrupt because they are betraying their fellow animals. The novel is ultimately about the way greed corrupts, and Orwell exposes the pigs as authoritarian rulers who use, terrify and even execute their so-called 'comrades' for their own gain. Orwell reveals their acts and their hypocrisy and the reader is led to abhor their behaviour and sympathise with those whose hopes they betray.

> **AO1** Convincing analytical response to task and text

How far the pigs abuse their authority is exemplified by the reduction of the original commandments to the single 'Four legs good, two legs better', and also by the way they alter the animals' memories of the original commandments. It is as if the revolution never happened. The animals face renewed hardships, so as 'Clover looked down the hillside her eyes filled with tears', and the reader responds sympathetically to Orwell's focus on her pain. Elsewhere, too, there is a contrast between the very basic conditions the animals endure and the luxurious lifestyle the pigs enjoy: 'Squealer was so fat that he could with difficulty see out of his eyes.' This image of bloated greed recalls the lifestyle of Stalin's inner circle in the Soviet Union.

> **AO4** Strong opening to paragraph; uses sentence variety well

> **AO1** Precise use of references

> **AO2** Explanation of writer's methods

> **AO3** Effective summative point

At times Orwell writes from the narrative viewpoint of the animals. So when they are 'Amazed, terrified, huddling together …', at the time of the executions, this triplet of verbs reveals their confusion and terror; when Orwell comments that 'the air was heavy with the smell of blood', that heaviness is exactly how it seems to the animals, as it weighs down on them and seems stifling. The reader is expected to reject what the pigs stand for and sympathise with the ordinary working animals.

> **AO2** Further exploration of effects of writer's methods

Throughout the novel, Boxer symbolises the honest working class while Napoleon represents the corrupt ruler. Boxer, of course, lacks the intelligence to see through the pigs' lies, so maintains his loyalty, believing 'Napoleon is always right'. His decency is set directly against Squealer's false emotions at the carthorse's departure in the van, which he describes as 'the most affecting sight I have ever seen!', and Napoleon's total betrayal of the revolution, in his toast: 'To the prosperity of the Manor Farm'. Orwell invites the reader to make judgements about the political implications of the pigs' machinations, demonstrating that power brings responsibility, but here it is grossly misused.

Paragraph 4

When the pigs actually turn into humans at the end, so 'it was impossible to say which was which', their corruption is inherent in Napoleon's words, their clothes and demeanour. Evil has triumphed and hope has been defeated. Orwell would expect the reader to reflect on Old Major's naivety when he states 'Man is the only real enemy we have' and proves with his tale that it is actually the abuse of power for personal gain that we should fear.

Paragraph 5

Check the skills

Re-read paragraphs four and five of this response and:

- think about what **additional points** you could make about how Napoleon betrays the revolution
- highlight any places where the student has shown **deeper insight** and offered **original or particularly thoughtful ideas** or made **interesting links**
- find any further references to **context**.

Now you try!

Now, using the plan you wrote for Question 10 on page 75, write a full response. Here is a reminder of the question:

10. What ideas about education does Orwell explore in the novel?
Write about:

- some ideas about education in the novel
- how Orwell presents these ideas to the reader.

[30 marks]

Now you try!

Now practise applying the skills you have learned to these four **new questions**.

- Note down the key points you wish to use.
- Select the key quotations you want to use from *Animal Farm*.
- Write your answer.
- Look at the list of key points for each question in the **Answers** (page 87).

16. 'Napoleon is cunning in the way he gradually takes complete control of the farm.'

How does Napoleon manage to take complete control of Animal Farm?
Write about:
- what Napoleon says and does
- how Orwell presents Napoleon's cunning.

[30 marks] AO4 [4 marks]

17. How are the two carthorses, Boxer and Clover, different?
Write about:
- the differences between Boxer and Clover
- how Orwell presents their differences.

[30 marks] AO4 [4 marks]

18. What happens to Old Major's dream of equality in *Animal Farm*?
Write about:
- Old Major's views on equality
- how Orwell presents the failure of Old Major's dream of equality.

[30 marks] AO4 [4 marks]

19. 'He carried a whip in his trotter.'

How far do the pigs use terror to maintain their hold over the other animals?
Write about:
- what the pigs do to terrorise the other animals
- how the pigs' actions and the animals' reactions are presented by Orwell.

[30 marks] AO4 [4 marks]

GLOSSARY

Literary or language terms	Explanation
allegory	a narrative, short story, poem or other work in which the characters or events are symbols that stand for ideas about life or society
anthropomorphic	a description of animals that are seen to behave like humans – they talk, for example
chronologically	events happening in order of time
cryptic	something short, puzzling and possibly ambiguous
detached style	impersonal, not emotionally involved
emotive	something that engages the emotions
empathy	imagining someone's feelings or experiences
evocative	making you feel, imagine or remember something
foreshadow	a warning or indication of a future event
ideology	a system of ideas on which an economic or political theory is based
imagery	descriptive language that uses images to make actions, objects and characters more vivid in the reader's mind
irony	deliberately saying one thing when you mean another, usually in a humorous, sarcastic or sometimes thoughtful way
mood	the tone or atmosphere created by an artistic work
narrative viewpoint	how a story is told; the point of view presented to the reader
omniscient	to know everything
oxymoron	a contradiction in terms, e.g. 'living death'
perspective	a view from a particular angle or an interpretation
propaganda	information, of a biased or misleading nature, promoting a political cause
rhetoric	language used for effect, e.g. a rhetorical question – asked for effect rather than for an answer
satire	a type of literature in which folly, evil or topical issues are held up to scorn through ridicule, irony or exaggeration
simile	when one thing is compared directly with another using 'like' or 'as'
symbol	something that represents something else, usually with meanings that are widely known (e.g. a dove as a symbol of peace)
tragedy	something sad, often involving death or suffering

ANSWERS

Note that the sample paragraphs given here provide only one possible approach to each task. Many other approaches would also be valid and appropriate.

PLOT AND STRUCTURE

Chapters 1 and 2 – Now you try! (page 7)

After Old Major dies, Snowball seems set to become leader as he has the most appealing personality: he is 'a more vivacious pig than Napoleon, quicker in speech and more inventive'. However, Napoleon rivals Snowball, as he has other attributes that set him apart. He is 'fierce-looking', and we are told he is used to getting his own way.

Chapters 3 and 4 – Now you try! (page 9)

Boxer fights bravely in the Battle of the Cowshed, but does not want to harm anyone and is distraught because he thinks he has killed the stable-lad. He says, 'I have no wish to take life'. Snowball, on the other hand, is unsentimental and cares only about victory: 'The only good human being is a dead one' in his view. The difference between their views of life is very clear.

Chapters 5 and 6 – Now you try! (page 11)

Boxer ignores the hardships, doing all the pigs could ask of him, and repeating his simple mantra 'I will work harder'. While the other animals work 60 hours a week, he starts each day before them. The labour, of course, fills his time and he does not have to try to work out what is going so wrong on the farm.

Chapters 7 and 8 – Now you try! (page 13)

Squealer skips around saying only positive things about Napoleon, so he is always referred to with respect as 'our leader, Comrade Napoleon' even after the dogs have carried out the executions. Also, Squealer claims that the pigs are not breaking the commandments. His lies mean that the pigs can get away with whatever they wish while the animals suffer under their regime of terror.

Chapters 9 and 10 – Now you try! (page 15)

By the end, Napoleon and the pigs have become just like the humans: 'it was impossible to say which was which'. Napoleon has become a brutal dictator, exploiting the animals and making everything even worse than it was in the time of Jones. Napoleon treats the humans as friends and changes the name back to 'Manor Farm'. His control is complete and his repressive regime has achieved its ends.

Form and structure – Now you try! (page 17)

Old Major's speech is ironic, because by the end of the novel the oppression is as bad as in Jones's time: 'The pigs ... all carried whips in their trotters.' The pigs have corrupted all the commandments. Animals have been killed and Boxer sold to the knacker. Ironically, the pigs abuse the animals as badly as Jones ever did, and although the farm has developed and been successful, the animals live under worse conditions than ever.

Quick quiz (pages 18–19)

1. Snowball, Napoleon and Squealer. 2. Napoleon and Snowball. 3. The Seven Commandments. 4. Boxer and Clover. 5. Jones, his men and others from Foxwood and Pinchfield farms. 6. 'Surely, comrades, you do not want Jones back?'. 7. He bans Sunday meetings. 8. Snowball. 9. Boxer. 10. Snowball. 11. The hens revolt. 12. Boxer defends Snowball's reputation. 13. Frederick and his men. 14. They get drunk. 15. A split hoof. 16. Squealer. 17. They buy whisky. 18. Sugarcandy Mountain. 19. They walk on two legs, carry whips, wear clothes, drink alcohol, etc. 20. By the end, everything is as bad as it was under Jones, if not worse.

Power paragraphs (page 19)

1. Old Major gives the animals hope but the pigs prove to be as greedy as the humans. The Commandments set out the guiding principles of Animalism, but they are all broken under Napoleon's regime as the world reverts to how it used to be. Indeed, the fact that by the end the sheep are bleating 'Four legs good, two legs better' demonstrates the revolution's total failure.

2. At the end, Napoleon dresses, walks and lives like a human. More importantly, he has the same views as them. He is proud to have overturned the ideals of the revolution, to have changed the farm back to the way it was and to symbolically change its name back to Manor Farm. The fact that 'the farm had grown richer without making the animals any richer' demonstrates his very human success.

Exam practice (page 19)

In the final paragraph, the animals who are watching through the window can see no difference between the humans and the pigs. This idea is the central message in the novel: that nothing seems to improve for ordinary people. Those in charge will always be equally cruel.

Even though there was a revolution on the farm, just like in the Soviet Union it failed in its objectives. The pigs resemble humans and behave like humans, and it is significant that those in the room are 'shouting in anger'. They continue to exhibit a violent attitude, even towards those for whom they claim to have 'friendly feelings'.

SETTING AND CONTEXT

Totalitarianism and Communism – Now you try! (page 21)

Under Napoleon's authoritarian leadership, the animals are treated cruelly and oppressively, so that the very air of the farm carries the scent of death: 'the air was heavy with the smell of blood'. It is an emotive description, intended to revolt the reader. Napoleon is a brutal fascist ruler who, just like Stalin, is prepared to carry out executions to maintain his power, and by the end the pigs even carry whips.

The Russian Revolution – Now you try! (page 23)

When Jones is driven out, the animals think their lives will be better and, indeed, at first 'All the animals capered with joy when they saw the whips going up in flames'. The word 'caper' shows their lightness of spirit – they do not realise that, ironically, the whips will return later, held in the pigs' trotters. Before the Russian Revolution, the people lived a miserable existence under the Tsar. The animals on Animal Farm were similarly exploited, so when Jones is driven out they believe their future is bright and that they will be working for themselves.

Quick quiz (page 25)

1. The Tsar. 2. Capitalism. 3. Animalism. 4. Napoleon. 5. The Soviet Union. 6. On the barn. 7. He led the army. 8. 'The life of an animal is misery and slavery'. 9. Near the cowshed and the windmill. 10. 'All animals are equal but some animals are more equal than others'.

Power paragraphs (page 25)

When the humans are driven out, the animals are initially overjoyed. Like the peasants in Russia, they celebrate and 'capered with joy when they saw the whips going up in flames'. They feel they have freedom and the farm belongs to them. 'Capered' pictures how they danced and rejoiced.

However, by the end the mood is very different. The animals' conditions are as bad as they ever were under Jones. They have learned to their cost that 'some animals are more equal than others', once again they live under fear of the whip, and as Napoleon celebrates in the farmhouse with their human neighbours, the animals are excluded, watching disconsolately – hopelessly – through the window.

CHARACTERS

Old Major – Now you try! (page 27)

The irony of the example Old Major gives, of Farmer Jones selling even Boxer – 'Jones will sell you to the knacker' – becomes evident once Boxer's age and split hoof prevent him working any longer for the pigs. They show no compassion and do exactly what Jones would have done. Old Major may identify the obvious problem for the animals: mankind ('Man is the only real enemy we have') but he does not realise that the weakest suffer in any system. He says that 'all animals are equal' – but he misunderstands, because some will always be more equal than others.

Snowball – Now you try! (page 29)

Orwell shows Snowball to have natural leadership qualities both in his planning before the battle and in his fearless actions. Indeed, 'Snowball flung his fifteen stone against Jones's legs'. The verb 'flung' demonstrates that he acts with full commitment and little regard for his own safety. At other times, he tries to help the farm's progress by promoting the ideals of Animalism, organising regular meetings to debate matters before making decisions, and establishing education for all.

Napoleon – Now you try! (page 31)

Although Napoleon does fight at the Battle of the Windmill, he deceives the animals with other claims about what he has done. For example, Squealer says, 'The windmill was … Napoleon's own creation.' Squealer always supports this idea that Napoleon is never wrong and therefore his failures, such as being duped by Frederick, are covered over. Orwell makes the reality clear to the reader but, for the animals, things are never Napoleon's fault.

Squealer – Now you try! (page 33)

Orwell reveals how devious Squealer is, as he uses emotive phrases to persuade the animals. At times, 'Squealer would talk with the tears running down his cheeks of Napoleon's wisdom'. He uses rhetoric too, in his pro-Napoleon propaganda: 'Surely, comrades, you do not want Jones back?' he asks. As a consummate liar, it seems Squealer can persuade anyone of anything. Orwell claims 'he could turn black into white', highlighting Squealer's deviousness through this use of opposites.

Boxer – Now you try! (page 35)

Boxer is dedicated to making the farm a success, but not at any cost because he does not want to hurt anyone: 'Who will believe that I did not do this on purpose?' His rhetorical question reveals his big heart. Even when the dogs attack him, rather than crushing them he looks to Napoleon for a sign of what he should do next. The farm relies on his strength, but he is sensitive too.

Clover and Benjamin – Now you try! (page 37)

Orwell conveys the impression that the long-lived Benjamin knows exactly what is going on: 'Benjamin … nodded his muzzle with a knowing air … but would say nothing'. 'Nodding' with a 'knowing air' makes him like an all-seeing wise person. Benjamin explains that donkeys, with their longevity, know that life will always be full of hardship, hunger and disappointment. The reader gains the impression that he expected the revolution to turn out as it did, but he keeps his thoughts to himself.

The other animals and humans – Now you try! (page 39)

Orwell demonstrates, through the ways in which the pigs use the sheep's bleating, how Napoleon manipulates the obedient animals. Initially, the sheep distract the animals from other ideas with their bleating of 'Four legs good, two legs bad'. Later, when it is necessary, they are taught to bleat that two legs are actually better. Meanwhile, they contrast with the dogs who terrorise the animals so that no one dare rebel against Napoleon, for fear of being executed.

Quick quiz (pages 40-1)

1. Seeing (and walking on two legs). 2. Benjamin. 3. 'I will work harder' and 'Napoleon is always right'. 4. Mollie. 5. Moses. 6. Benjamin. 7. Berkshire boar. 8. 'The only good human being is a dead one'. 9. Squealer. 10. Frederick. 11. The cat. 12. Napoleon. 13. 'All men are enemies. All animals are comrades'. 14. Mr. Whymper. 15. The man driving the knacker's van. 16. Clover. 17. Clover learns the whole alphabet. 18. Winston Churchill. 19. 'Beasts of England'. 20. His own way.

Power paragraphs (page 41)

1. The majority of the animals support the revolution, but Orwell picks out the characteristics of those who do not. Mollie, for example, who represents the self-centred elite, likes her ribbons and being petted by humans, and asks: 'Will there still be sugar after the Revolution?' That is significant because sugar masks the taste of things that might be unpleasant. Of course, she benefited under Jones's stewardship of the farm, and soon leaves to resume her pampered former life.

2. It is not enough for Napoleon to have Squealer's propaganda working for him: the dogs supply the threat to keep the animals in order. They work like Stalin's secret police, making the animals frightened and executing any who might offer opposition: 'the dogs promptly tore their throats out'. With this savagery ('tore'), they protect Napoleon and the pigs – which is why they are rewarded.

Exam practice (page 41)

Orwell shows that Frederick and Pilkington do have things in common, such as their greed. Each, for example, wants to 'turn Jones's misfortune to his own advantage'. When they begin to fear the revolution might be successful they spread rumours that at Animal Farm the animals 'tortured one another with red-hot horseshoes' and 'had their females in common'. The details Orwell includes – for the horrors they invent – indicates the corrupted nature of their characters.

However, they are also different. Frederick, who is supposed to be like Hitler, is 'a tough, shrewd man', the terse language indicating his personality. Orwell contrasts him with Pilkington, representing Churchill; he likes 'fishing or hunting' and is a gentleman farmer whose farm is in 'a disgraceful condition'. The implication is that although they sit in the Red Lion with Jones, and are contrasting versions of humanity, neither has much sympathy for him because of their own selfishness.

THEMES

Power and corruption – Now you try! (page 43)

By the end of the novel, the pigs are as corrupt as Jones, Pilkington and Frederick, even dressing similarly, as 'Napoleon himself appeared in a black coat, rat-catcher breeches, and leather leggings'. Orwell makes him sound like a country gentleman who dines and celebrates with the humans. Napoleon has reversed all the changes introduced after the revolution, even altering the flag and the name of the farm, and it is significant that Pilkington praises Napoleon for treating his animals so badly.

Freedom and equality – Now you try! (page 45)

By the end of the novel, the one remaining commandment no longer states that all animals are equal but reads as the oxymoron: 'All animals are equal but some animals are more equal than others'. This new meaning is evident in the contrasting lifestyles of the pigs and the other animals. The pigs have become fat, living a life of luxury in the house, while outside the animals work harder and eat less, mirroring the failure of the revolution in the Soviet Union.

Oppression and violence – Now you try! (page 47)

When the executions take place, Orwell shows how the animals are cowed into submission by Napoleon's violence, which extends even to pigs when 'the dogs … seized four of the pigs by the ear and dragged them, squealing with pain, to Napoleon's feet'. The onomatopoeia of 'squealing' makes the scene particularly disturbing. However, this is not the only indication of violence under Napoleon: the pigs all carry whips by the end and his snarling dogs are a permanent threat.

Education and learning – Now you try! (page 49)

After Old Major explains his dream, the pigs begin to learn by using an old spelling book, and soon 'they could … read and write perfectly'. This enables Snowball to begin the education of the animals, to design the windmill and read about the campaigns of Julius Caesar so he can plan the farm's defence.

Language and propaganda – Now you try! (page 51)

Squealer has a range of persuasive techniques, but his use of rhetorical questions such as 'Surely, comrades, you do not want Jones back?' is one of the most powerful tools. It does not give the animals any power to reply. He also uses this approach when they need to be convinced of anything, such as when Squealer declares Snowball is 'no better than a criminal' or when somebody tries to remind the others of Snowball's bravery in the Battle of the Cowshed.

Community – Now you try! (page 53)

In contrast to the earlier ideals of equality in their community, Orwell shows the animals' shock when Napoleon has animals executed: 'The animals huddled about Clover, not speaking'. The choice of the word 'huddle' emphasises their togetherness but also their need for some kind of comfort. This verb is repeated, when Napoleon first emerges with a whip (Chapter 10). In their confusion and terror, they once again close ranks.

Quick quiz (page 54)

1. 'Our leader, Comrade Napoleon'. 2. Outside, looking through the window. 3. They have brass studs. 4. Four. 5. Benjamin and Muriel, the goat. 6. Snowball. 7. From a book: *Electricity for Beginners.* 8. 'files, reports, minutes, and memoranda'. 9. He fires his gun. 10. They bleat 'Four legs good, two legs better'. 11. Moses, Mollie and the cat. 12. See Squealer's list of the ways life is better in Chapter 9 of the novel. 13. A goose. 14. The smell of blood. 15. 'Beasts of England'. 16. It is taken from the post in the garden and Napoleon has it buried. 17. They grow fat, they walk on two legs and their faces look like those of the humans. 18. He blames someone else – usually Snowball, sometimes the humans. 19. The discipline, the long working hours and the low rations for the animals. 20. Benjamin.

Power paragraphs (page 55)

1. Jones drinks heavily. He does not look after the animals properly and Old Major tells them: 'every one of you will scream your lives out at the block within a year'. They are underfed as the farm falls into disrepair, reflecting the neglect of Russia under the Tsar. On the day of the Rebellion, the animals have not been fed all day, but when they help themselves to food Jones and his men attack them with whips.

2. After the revolution, the animals taste freedom. The next morning, they race out to gaze all around them – at the land that now belongs to them: 'The animals were happy as they had never conceived it was possible to be.' The language is joyful and uplifting, as their hopes seem to have been realised. Because the farm is now theirs, they enjoy their labour as they have never done before and, working together, produce the most successful harvest ever.

Exam practice (page 55)

At the end of the novel, it seems that all the gains of the revolution have been lost. Napoleon does not want to stir rebellion ('Nothing could be further from the truth'). There is clear irony in his use of the word 'truth', after all the lies the animals have been told. He says he now wants business relationships with his neighbours and all signs of change have gone: the use of 'comrade' has been suppressed, Old Major's skull has been buried, there will be no more marches and the farm flag is changed.

His corruption is plain to see as he shows how human-like he has become. By pointing out that he and the other pigs own the farm, he dismisses the claims of the other animals, and by removing all signs of the revolution – which was intended to produce equality – he demonstrates his rejection of the revolution's aims. In offering a toast 'To the prosperity of the Manor Farm', he turns back the clock to how the farm was under Mr Jones and puts an end to the other animals' dreams.

LANGUAGE

Imagery and vocabulary – Now you try! (page 57)

To reveal how the animals are oppressed, Orwell uses a recurring simile: 'the animals worked like slaves'. This image emphasises the brutality of their existence and their lack of freedom. Orwell uses it when the farm adopts a 60-hour week, and the phrase echoes through the text as the animals face starvation and contrasts with the positive, evocative vocabulary used immediately after the revolution: 'they cropped mouthfuls of the sweet summer grass'. The idea of 'cropping' makes it sound plentiful, 'sweet' appeals to the senses and the alliteration of 'sweet summer' sounds soft and pleasant.

Narrative style – Now you try! (page 59)

Orwell shows that the animals are as excluded at the end as they were at the start, placing them outside the celebration, and we see through their eyes how they 'tiptoed up to the house, and … peered in at the dining-room window'. The verb 'tiptoed' emphasises their fear and 'peered in' makes it seem as if they are nervous, frightened of what they might see. In recognising their fear, we sympathise with them.

Quick quiz (page 61)

1. 'A Fairy Tale'. 2. It makes the animals think they are all part of an equal community. 3. Omniscient. 4. Clover's thoughts. 5. Chronological. 6. 'Amazed, terrified, huddling together'. 7. Vocabulary that makes you feel, imagine or remember something. 8. Old Major says what Jones will do – but that is exactly what the pigs do later. 9. The demonstrations are planned, so cannot be spontaneous. 10. Just after the revolution: optimistic/happy/amazed; at the end of the novel: disillusioned/frightened/confused.

Power paragraphs (page 61)

Squealer uses rhetoric to win round the animals whenever they need to be persuaded. So, for example, he uses the repeated question, 'Surely, comrades, you do not want Jones back?' and he knows it will produce an immediate response of 'no' in their minds. 'Surely' demands they agree with him, and 'comrade' emphasises the fact that they are all in it together.

At other times, though, he has a different approach, introducing language to baffle his listeners; terms from the business world, like 'files' and 'memoranda', to make what the pigs are doing seem difficult and, obviously, beyond what the animals could manage. (Boxer, symbolising the working classes, only has the ability to remember four letters of the alphabet.) Thus Squealer uses the vocabulary of business to make the animals realise how much they need the pigs' intelligence and transactional skills.

EXAM PRACTICE

Planning your character response – Now you try! (page 67)

Paragraph 1: Snowball is a lively and attractive personality/effective communicator/learns to read and plans

Paragraph 2: He sets up Animal Committees, his role in Battle of Cowshed, planning for the windmill

Paragraph 3: How he is driven out, clear differences with Napoleon; his lies about Snowball

Paragraph 4: Napoleon's deeds in contrast to Snowball's, reversing his positive changes

Paragraph 5: Snowball is shown not to be perfect (e.g. he thinks killing and milk and apples for pigs both acceptable) but Orwell expects reader to compare him favourably with Napoleon

ANSWERS

Grade 5 annotated answer – Check the skills (page 69)

Points: Boxer's loyalty and hard work, even when injured. Never blames Napoleon. Para 5 – Tragic irony of his end

Context: Workers' loyalty to leaders in revolution … workers betrayed by leaders

Interpretation: 'we empathise', 'tragic ending', 'ironic'

Exam practice – Now you try! (page 69)

Boxer fights for the farm too in a fearless way. He is awarded 'Animal Hero, First Class' after the Battle of the Windmill and leads the fight at the Battle of the Cowshed. This helps save Animal Farm. He knocks out the stable-lad, even though it upsets him to do it. This makes the other men flee. He also hits several men on the head when Frederick attacks in the Battle of the Windmill. Orwell tells us this to show Boxer as a selfless hero.

Grade 7 annotated answer – Check the skills (page 71)

Well-expressed ideas: 'a kind of propaganda tool for them', 'he does lose his life – for nothing more than a case of whisky'

Deeper insights: 'in its blind obedience, is actually of enormous value to the pigs', 'He never loses heart, but …'

Context: 'he works as the pigs doubtless want every animal to work', 'like model labourers on the collective farms in the Soviet Union'

Grade 7 annotated answer – Now you try! (page 71)

Indicative content for a full response:

AO1:

- He reads books to learn how to make the farm a success
- Plans the windmill; establishes education and committees
- Leads in the Battle of the Cowshed
- Is vivacious and a natural leader
- Thinks the only good human being is a dead one/ does not complain about the milk and apples incident

AO2:

- Contrast with Napoleon: 'vivacious', 'more inventive' – positive descriptions
- 'Snowball flung his fifteen stone against Jones's legs' – 'flung' shows commitment, no care for own safety
- Driven out, he 'was seen no more' – very final
- Increasingly used symbolically to frighten the animals, and held responsible for everything that goes wrong – which sheds more light on the corruption of the pigs
- His name suggests purity but likely to melt, no ultimate power

AO3:

- Like Trotsky/Lenin, he makes the farm, initially, a wonderful place for the animals to enjoy
- Is part of larger picture – how revolution turns from his positivity to corruption of Napoleon
- But would Snowball have remained 'good', because power corrupts? He enjoys the same privileges as the other pigs

Planning your theme response – Now you try! (page 75)

Paragraph 1: The pigs have control because of their knowledge/ability to read and write. Squealer's use of language

Paragraph 2: What Snowball achieves through his learning: windmill plans, battle plans, farming knowledge: education as a positive

Paragraph 3: Snowball's failed attempts to educate the animals. How the animals struggle to read. Clear divide between animals and pigs

Paragraph 4: Pigs able to manipulate commandments/ deal with humans/read newspapers: all presented as part of pigs' corruption

Paragraph 5: Summary: education for workers vital for their protection, so they are not exploited (lacking education leads them to accept the corruption of their revolution)

Grade 5 annotated answer – Check the skills (page 77)

Points: Napoleon like Jones – carries whip/gets drunk

Interpretation: 'This all makes us see …', 'This is intended to shock the reader …', 'This is to make us realise …'

Context: 'farm is unchanged', 'revolution has failed'

Grade 5 annotated answer – Now you try (page 77)

At times Orwell writes from the narrative viewpoint of the animals. So when they are 'Amazed, terrified, huddling together …', at the time of the executions, this triplet of verbs reveals their confusion and terror; when Orwell comments that 'the air was heavy with the smell of blood', that heaviness is exactly how it seems to the animals, as it weighs down on them and seems stifling. The reader is expected to reject what the pigs stand for and sympathise with the ordinary working animals.

Grade 7 annotated answer – Check the skills (page 79)

Well-expressed ideas: Napoleon's betrayal: animals killed, breaking other commandments including drinking alcohol, selling Boxer, trading with humans, turning farm back to the way it used to be

Deeper insight: 'His decency can be set directly against Squealer's false emotions'; 'Orwell would expect the reader to reflect on Old Major's naivety'; 'their corruption is inherent in …'

Context: 'Orwell invites the reader to make judgements about the political implications of the pigs' machinations'; 'Evil has triumphed and hope has been defeated'; 'proves with his tale that it is actually the abuse of power for personal gain that we should fear …'

Grade 7 annotated answer – Now you try! (page 79)

Indicative content for a full response:

AO1:

- It puts the pigs in a position of power – they are able to manipulate the animals, change the commandments …
- Squealer's deceit – 'I could show you this in his own writing, if you were able to read it'
- What pigs learn enables them to run and develop the farm, e.g. Snowball learns from *Electricity for Beginners*
- Snowball's activities might have produced a more cooperative society
- Without adequate language, animals cannot express their thoughts
- More education would be a boon – pigs tricked by Frederick

AO2:

- Orwell makes clear the first thing Napoleon does is ban Snowball's cooperative activities
- Corruption revealed by Squealer's use of complicated language the animals do not understand: 'files', 'memoranda'
- Legal education, in the form of Whymper, criticised by Orwell ('a sly-looking little man') – small in spirit too, and 'sly' suggests evil
- Pigs' transformation into humans symbolised by reading *Daily Mirror*

AO3:

- Novel proves that 'knowledge is power'
- The farm is developed, e.g. the windmill – through the benefits of education
- The farm represents the collective farms in the Soviet Union – successful, but not for the uneducated workers
- Education initially a policy post-revolution, but rulers actually do not want an educated population, because education produces ideas and can prompt opposition

Practice questions – Character question 16 (page 80)

Indicative content for a full response:

AO1:

- He drives out Snowball
- He uses the dogs to frighten and Squealer to persuade
- He changes the commandments to the pigs' advantage
- He consolidates his position by removing the changes brought in after the revolution

AO2:

- Projects himself as 'our leader, Comrade Napoleon': emphasis on who is in charge

- After Snowball's departure, mounts 'the raised portion of the floor where Old Major had previously stood' ('raised' shows his position and, significantly, he replaces Old Major)
- Increasingly presented as a superior, distant figure, with Squealer acting for him
- Napoleon symbolically wears clothes and carries a whip

AO3:

- Mirrors the takeover of Russia by Stalin
- Secret police and propaganda were Communist tools
- Trading relationships established with previous enemies, just like in the Soviet Union
- Cult of personality develops, replacing the pure aims of the revolution

Practice questions – Character question 17 (page 80)

Indicative content for a full response:

AO1:

- Boxer the workhorse, Clover the motherly figure (e.g. protects ducklings)
- Boxer strong supporter of Napoleon, Clover cares for Boxer's welfare
- Boxer works extra hours, responsible for the heavy work in construction of the windmills and plays significant parts in battles
- Clover survives into a sad old age, watching and trying to remember how things were
- Boxer taken by the knacker, Clover unable to save him

AO2:

- They are 'the most faithful disciples of the revolution': as if they have religious fervour
- Boxer's simple thought processes reflected in simple language: 'It must be due to some fault in ourselves'
- Clover's 'eyes filled with tears': emotive, tragic language
- Boxer shown as a confused animal in a van as he is taken; in contrast, Orwell foregrounds Clover's reflections, e.g. her thoughts after the executions and at the end

AO3:

- Boxer represents the working class, unable to learn beyond four letters
- Boxer is exploited, as Stalin exploited the workers
- Clover is also of the working class but represents caring and goodness, which has no value to Napoleon
- The workers demonstrate loyalty to those in charge, but do not get the rewards they deserve
- Workers can be removed, sold, once their usefulness is at an end – as shown by the sale of Boxer

ANSWERS

Practice questions – Theme question 18 (page 80)

Indicative content for a full response:

AO1:

- Old Major states that man exploits animals: 'Man is the only real enemy we have' (taking their products, selling them to the knacker)
- Without man, there will be no hunger or overwork
- 'All animals are equal'
- 'Beasts of England' sums up his beliefs

AO2:

- Hierarchy revealed even at Old Major's meeting: 'the pigs settled down … in front of the platform' p1 – their symbolic place
- Dream of equality fails as commandments gradually eroded, becoming the final oxymoron: 'All animals are equal but some animals are more equal than others'
- Pigs replace men (their power represented by terror, whips, exploitation)
- 'perfect unity, perfect comradeship' – irony, since what happens is so far from the repeated 'perfection'

AO3:

- Old Major's pure philosophy is manipulated by the pigs for their own ends
- The novel exposes the horrors of the Russian Revolution, from seizure of power to violent purges and suppression of dissent
- We learn that the problem is not humans but 'selfishness and greed'
- The clear message, mirroring what happened in the Soviet Union, is that 'some animals will always be more equal than others'

Practice questions – Theme question 19 (page 80)

Indicative content for a full response:

AO1:

- Dogs used to terrify the animals and suppress any opposition
- Hens starved into submission, and hence a warning to others
- Executions are a shock ('the air was heavy with the smell of blood'), but also a threat
- Animals accept Squealer's explanations and remain positive even after the executions, believing at first that their lives are still better than under Jones
- Pigs carry whips by the end
- Snowball used as a shadowy threat to help maintain control

AO2:

- 'the dogs … seized four of the pigs by the ear and dragged them, squealing with pain, to Napoleon's feet': violence inherent in verbs
- Squealer's false tears, symbolic of the pigs' duplicity ('Squealer would talk with the tears running down his cheeks of Napoleon's wisdom'), make the real suffering seem even worse
- After the executions: 'The animals huddled around Clover, not speaking' – power of 'huddled', as if needing protection; 'not speaking' because they cannot find words
- The pigs' 'discipline' praised by Pilkington – but might be seen as a condemnation from Orwell

AO3:

- Life on the farm does not improve: animals still overworked and starved, just as in the Soviet Union
- Executions represent Stalin's purges, dogs represent Stalin's secret police
- On the farm, as in Russia, violence achieves its objectives